P9-AGS-675

Withdrawn from

American Jewelry

Glamour and Tradition

Penny Proddow

Debra Healy

Photographs by David Behl

Foreword by Ralph Esmerian

RIZZOLI
NEW YORK

Copyright © 1987 by Office du Livre, S.A., Fribourg, Switzerland
Published in 1987 in the United States of America by:
Rizzoli International Publications, Inc.
597 Fifth Avenue / New York 10017

All rights reserved.
No part of this book may be reproduced in any manner
whatsoever without permission of Rizzoli International Publications, Inc.

This book was printed in July, 1987 by Dai Nippon Printing Co. Ltd., Tokyo.
Typesetting: Trufont Typographers, Inc., Hicksville, NY.
Binding and photolithographs: Dai Nippon Printing Co. Ltd., Tokyo.
Design: Homans Design, Inc., New York, NY.
Production: Emma Staffelbach.
Editorial coordination: Barbara Perroud-Benson.

Library of Congress Cataloging-in-Publication Data

Proddow, Penny.
  American jewelry.
  Bibliography: p.
  Includes index.
  1. Jewelry—United States—History.   I. Healy, Debra.
II. Title.
NK7312.P76   1987   739.27'0973   87-83
ISBN 0-8478-0830-0

Printed and bound in Japan

Frontispiece

1. 18th-Century Style Necklace
1977

Natural black button pearls,
diamonds, and platinum
Manufactured by George Peyrot,
Inc. for R. Esmerian, Inc.

Front cover
Commemorative Watch
Early 20th century
See page 60, Plate **35**.

Back Cover
Two Flower Brooches
Early 1940s
See page 123, Plate **97**.

C1

Contents

Acknowledgments and Photo Credits

The authors would like to thank the following people, as well as private collectors, for their help, encouragement, and permission to photograph their jewelry: Joseph Alfano, formerly of Verdura, Inc.; Claude Arpels and Veronique Ma'Arop of Van Cleef & Arpels, Inc.; Nicolas Bongard and Steve Collins of Jean Schlumberger; Nicola Bulgari of Bulgari, New York; André Chervin of Carvin French, Inc.; Julius Cohen of Julius Cohen, Inc.; Mary Corliss of the Film Stills Archive at the Museum of Modern Art; Robert Kaufmann of the Costume Institute at the Metropolitan Museum of Art; François Curiel of Christie's; Ralph Esmerian of R. Esmerian, Inc.; Jacqueline Fay of Sotheby's; Paul Flato; Robert Gibson of Raymond C. Yard, Inc.; Paul Henry of Greenleaf & Crosby; the Heyman family of Oscar Heyman & Bros, Inc.; Laurence Krashes of Harry Winston, Inc.; Ward Landrigan of Verdura, Inc.; Hans Nadelhoffer; Grant Peacock of Grant Peacock, Inc. (formerly of Charlton & Co.); Dudley Ramsden; Walter Scheer and Mrs. William Scheer; Bonnie Selfe of Cartier, Inc., New York; Stanley Silberstein of David Webb, Inc.; Annamarie V. Sandecki of N.W. Ayer Inc. Archives; the Tamis family of Louis Tamis & Son; Patricia Vaill of Seaman Schepps; Francois Verger; Janet Zapata of the Tiffany & Co. Archives; Russel Zelenetz and Steven Feuerman of Fred Leighton, Trump Tower.

Delphin Broussailles, Lily Cates, Edward Lee Cave, the late Victor Conrad, Dan Davis, Aldo del Noce, I.B. Dobry, Rachelle Epstein, Charles Flynn, Maurice Galle, Hilda Janssens, David Jones, Sarah Kutas, Anthony Lent, William Luckey, Alfred Montezinos, Dorothea Peterson, Charles M. Newton, Margaret Schorsch, Maurice Semensohn, Stephanie Stein, John Ullmann, and Jack and Joan Quinn.

We would also like to thank our many friends for their useful insights; the conclusions in the book, however, are our own.

Foreword

Travel the world; observe the customs and traditions of different societies; look back through centuries; peer into ancient civilizations—you will find that jewelry is the oldest and the most universal of symbols. It is a language capable of conveying the passions and emotions that exist on a personal level between two human beings, while signifying the wealth and rank of individuals on a more public stage.

No matter the place or historic time, a man gives a woman a jewel to enhance and complement her beauty. More importantly, the jewel has become an expression of his pride in and his love for her. Jewelry has always been a silent symbol, the beautiful witness to this basic human celebration. Indeed, in many societies the mere exchange of rings can express the social and legal union of a couple.

In the more formal arena of history, jewels were made for rulers of the state and for princes of the church, to commemorate their temporal power and authority. As late as the twentieth century, the maharajahs of India bedecked themselves with torsades of pearls and precious stones to proclaim the pomp and authority of their title. The pharaohs of Egypt went one step beyond and commissioned jewelry for the next life, with which they would be buried.

With the emergence of a strong middle class in the industrial West during the nineteenth and twentieth centuries, more and more jewelry was made as trappings for the new rich. Jewelry was no longer the exclusive symbol of the court and the church; portable and highly visible, it became a prerequisite of the new merchant class.

The universal and timeless appeal of jewelry is also due to its size—which fits perfectly with human limbs. It is comfortable to wear. There is nothing hostile or forbidding about the nature of a jewel. As a benevolent appendage of the body and the emotions, it defines a person's taste and spirit. Forever tenable and portable, a jewel remains a physical source of security and confidence.

Look upon a jewel, and wonder at the magical and romantic union of Earth and Man: stone and metal transformed and shaped by ingenuity and craft. Depending upon the quality of the artist-jeweler's vision, eyes, and hands, a jewel may become a work of art. As a gift it will symbolize a relationship forever; worn as a badge, it can indicate material wealth and social rank. Yet, in addition, jewelry will speak the language of its creators, the team of artisans who seek to transmit their vision of beauty, not on a painted canvas or a free-standing sculpture, but in a much more personal work of art—a jewel to adorn the human body.

How ironic that the names of relatively few of the craftsmen who created this universal art form are known today. True, it is possible for a single individual to design and then to make a piece of jewelry, but historically creating jewelry is seldom the act of a lone designer-artisan. The concept for a piece may emanate from a jewelry merchant, a designer, or from the head of a workshop. Under his guidance and authority, the implementation will be in the anonymous hands of lapidaries, model makers, casters, jewelers, enamelers, setters, engravers, and polishers. Alone, each craftsman is rich in skill and pride but unable to complete a piece of jewelry; together, with discipline and interaction, a team that will create fine jewelry can be formed.

Although the best workshops for making precious jewelry have been located in western Europe since the Renaissance, ironically, many of the design traditions and methods of using materials are rooted in Middle and Far Eastern cultures. European merchants and jewelers traveled to India for four centuries in search of Indian and Mogul pieces, rich in stones and arabesque design. Voyages to the Far East were necessitated by the abundance on the Asian continent of the raw materials that Europe lacked. Apart from jade, rubies, sapphires, emeralds, and pearls from the ocean, the first and only diamond mines in the world (until the discovery of Brazilian diamonds in the eighteenth century) were in India. Other Eastern influences emerged from archeological excavations in Egypt and Greece, which inspired a contemporary style of ancient jewelry during the nineteenth and twentieth centuries. It must be borne in mind that European jewelers voluntarily sought out and assimilated these Eastern motifs to form their own creations. In doing so, they were inadvertently preparing themselves to export and pass on a Western jewelry tradition.

With the colonization and independence of the United States of America, jewelers from Europe came to the New World bringing their traditional skills and values to that marketplace. There was no jewelry establishment to join, no workshops or guilds for which to qualify. As with all other trades and professions on the American continent, jewelry had to make a fresh start: emulating Old World styles and standards on the one hand, creating designs and pieces generated by the fresh spirit of the young country on the other.

For the first time in a nation's social and cultural development, the beginnings of a jewelry tradition were linked to the growth of a working middle class. Gone were kings and courts, popes and churches; in their place was an industrial society composed of free individuals. At first, American jewelry design followed the more modest of the European styles. Gradually, as the country prospered, more jewelers came to the new land in search of freedom from European authoritarianism and traditions. An American style of jewelry was born; the story begins.

Ralph Esmerian   New York City

Introduction

After calling himself a "jack of all trades,"[1] in 1879 an anonymous jeweler defined the jewelry industry in nineteenth-century America: ". . . it is not uncommon to find men that are skilled in half a dozen trades. The jewelry business combines half a dozen or more different branches, each of which in European countries is practiced as a distinct and separate industry. Here, however, the practical jeweler is supposed to be a watchmaker, an engraver, a mender of trinkets, a good salesman, and not infrequently a designer, and very often an inventor and patentee.

"Indeed, if he is also a proprietor of a retail store he is expected to know how to do these things, buy and sell all kinds of goods, and to have an intimate knowledge regarding each and all of them. There is something in the atmosphere of America that breeds enterprise."[2]

This is a study of one aspect of American enterprise—the production of fine jewelry, which began in the workrooms and shops of these early tinkerers. Americans' esteem for precious jewelry grew with the economic development of their nation. Jewelry houses multiplied and prospered as Americans made their fortunes.

Shortly after the Civil War jewelers were surprised to find a growing preference among their patrons for precious stones of exceptional quality. Wealthy Americans were now willing to pay for the best, and their standards were high. The most desired settings were made of gold, platinum, and upon occasion, silver. A respect for unique productions, where workmanship, materials, and design converged, existed in America in the flush of postwar prosperity.

The country was big and wide open. There was ready employment for those with jeweler's and watchmaker's skills. By the end of the nineteenth century, craftsmen whose families had traditionally worked under the patronage of royalty began to choose to emigrate to America. This insured the success of the developing jewelry industry.

This history of American jewelry has been mostly limited to signed jewels. There were many jewelry firms in America, but only a small number consistently signed their pieces. In retrospect, those that did proved the most prominent in early trade journals and newspapers. We have been most fortunate in being able to handle such jewels while studying and selecting the pieces illustrated.

In each period we encountered the influence of fashion dictating change and, at times, almost total destruction: most precious jewelry was broken up, and its metals and materials applied to new styles. Early jewelry that has survived was saved by individuals for sentimental reasons.

Our history ends with some exceptional examples of modern precious jewelry, chosen to illustrate the ongoing American tradition.

Penny Proddow   **Debra Healy**   New York City

Chapter One

Early American Jewelry Establishments
North, East, South, and West

Early American Jewelry

2. Miniature
Late 18th century, Connecticut

Patriotic jewel depicting Lady Liberty
Painted ivory and gold
Inscribed on back, "Lady Liberty
Alijah Canfield   April 1797"
Unsigned

3. Miniatures
Late 18th century, New England
Unsigned

Mourning locket depicting family with
funerary urn
Painted ivory and yellow gold
Inscribed on urn, "Prepare for Death
and follow me."

Friendship pin depicting clasped
hands
Painted ivory and gilt pinchbeck
Inscribed, "Friendship the fountain of
love."

The first American jewelry reflected the character of colonial America, which was heavily influenced by the immigration of large numbers of English Protestants. These staunch settlers, with their great respect for education, law, and religious freedom, were craftsmen as well as farmers, traders, doctors, lawyers, members of the clergy, and schoolteachers. Sometimes whole communities had emigrated together, bringing with them a common set of values. Part of the outlook of these settlers included a utilitarian approach to knowledge—they felt it should be directed toward providing for basic human needs rather than toward the creation of unnecessary luxuries. Americans of a later period would, as a result, be forced to look to Europe to fulfill their more frivolous desires.

The pioneer members of the jewelry trade worked in small workshops and foundries and manufactured objects of a practical and sentimental nature, which were unostentatious in design. Most towns had a small jewelry shop that sold wedding rings, knee buckles, shoe buckles, stone buttons, plain gold-bead necklaces, lockets, gold thimbles, and snuff boxes. These stock items became more elaborate with time.

American settlers with money to spend could afford the more valuable objects in silver and gold; the rest contented themselves with pinchbeck, pewter, brass, or steel. (Pinchbeck, an alloy of zinc and copper that resembles gold, had been invented by the London watchmaker Christopher Pinchbeck in 1670.) Some jewelry was set with genuine stones, including garnets, Brazil topazes and, in some cases, with diamond brilliants and rose diamonds. Less valuable pieces were set with glass stones and paste. An article with any stone setting at all was immediately put into a higher price category. Jewelry was imported from the continent, but only in styles compatible with New World sobriety.

The American Revolution of 1776 set the scene for the establishment of a federal government and for the growth of mercantile prosperity.

The first jewels made by the new nation's jewelers and goldsmiths were commemorative pieces for everyman: Washington memorial lockets, brooches, and rings, as well as mourning jewelry for those who had fallen in battle. A painted pendant from this period depicts the goddess Liberty performing a victory dance.

The Founding of Shreve, Crump & Low Co.
Boston, Massachusetts

At a time when the battles of Concord, Lexington, and Bunker Hill were still fresh in the country's memory, the watchmaker John McFarlane left Salem, Massachusetts, to set himself up in business in Boston.

John McFarlane's shop at 51 Marlborough Street (which was underway in 1769) was a novelty shop—said by some today to be the forerunner of all jewelry establishments in America. These shops sold watches and by necessity repaired them; as an extra attraction, they displayed the latest novelties.

Shipping was the major industry in the state of Massachusetts. Since it benefited from low tariffs and tonnage duties, it provided transport for every type of product. McFarlane's venture was dependent in part for its stock on imported goods brought back by Yankee traders. McFarlane prospered; in 1809 he bought another firm, Fletcher &Gardner. His entire business was acquired in 1813 by Jabez Baldwin, a goldsmith and silversmith.

Baldwin and his two partners, John Jones and a Mr. Ward, were also from Salem. The association between McFarlane's seventeen-year-old firm and the active city of Salem continued with John J. Low, the descendant of a sea-going family. John worked as an apprentice to Jabez Baldwin and became a partner in 1822. (John's son George would later form Shreve, Crump & Low Co.)

Reflecting the speed of development throughout America, the Baldwin & Jones firm changed partners at least six times between 1822 and 1840: Putnam & Low (1822), John J. Low & Co., John B. Jones Co., Jones, Low & Ball; Low, Ball & Co., and Jones, Ball & Poor (1840).

Unlike the staid jewelry houses of Europe, the young American firms changed partners and locations constantly—an indication of how adaptive these enterprises really were. The unifying element in the case of Shreve, Crump & Low Co. was the adventurous spirit of Salem's inhabitants: the firm's partners and associates shared a common heritage with the town's sea-going families.

The Shreve Family

Benjamin Shreve (1813–96), son of a well-known Salem sea captain, moved from Salem, where he was born, to Saco, Maine, in 1828. There he learned the jeweler's trade and established his own enterprise, producing small jewelry of a sentimental nature. The seaports of Maine were prosperous in those days due to the thriving fishing and lumber industries. Benjamin went from Saco to New York, where he worked with Tarbox & Kingsley (which became Kingsley & Shreve of 22 Maiden Lane, New York [1853]). He joined Jones, Ball & Poor (which became Jones, Shreve, Brown & Co. [1855], Shreve, Brown & Co. [1857], and Shreve, Stanwood & Co. [1860–9]) in 1853, and the next year Commodore Perry signed a trade treaty with Japan. The firm of Shreve, Brown & Co., with its long tradition of Salem seafaring men, would profit greatly from the China trade.

George C. Shreve
Shreve & Co., San Francisco, California

George C. Shreve (1828–93) was Benjamin Shreve's half-brother, fifteen years his junior, and served as his apprentice in Saco, Maine. Later he followed Benjamin to New York and joined him at Kingsley & Shreve. Earlier in his life George had already been to sea with another brother, Samuel, as a sailor on an Atlantic coasting vessel.

Motivated by the potential profits from the California Gold Rush, Samuel and George sailed for San Francisco in 1852 by way of Cape Horn; they set up their jewelry business immediately. Later, Samuel was drowned near the Isthmus of Panama and, according to an agreement between the brothers, the survivor inherited the other's entire estate. With the help of his brother's assets, George Shreve made Shreve & Co. of San Francisco its finest jewelry retailer, prospering as the fortunes of the American West grew.

Major William P. Shreve
Shreve, Crump & Low Co.

William P. Shreve (1835–1919) was also born in Salem. He started his jewelry career in New York with Henry Ginnel of Maiden Lane, an importer of watches. In 1858, William sailed to San Francisco to join his brother Samuel and was associated with him for two years before returning east on the *Zephyr* by way of Cape Horn with Captain King of Salem.

At the outbreak of the Civil War, William joined the Ninth New York Militia and then transferred to the Second United States Sharp Shooters in Washington, D.C. He fought at the crucial battles of Antietam and Gettysburg. Having completed his wartime duties with the rank of major, William returned to Boston. In 1865 he took a partner and formed Shreve, Stanwood & Co. In 1869 the firm became Shreve, Crump & Low, and in 1888 it incorporated with Major Shreve as its treasurer. He retired just a few months before his death in 1919.

Throughout his business career, William Shreve kept up his interest in the Civil War: he wrote on military history, served as an officer of the Loyal Legion, and was associated with the Boston Historical Society.

Charles H. Crump
Shreve, Crump & Low Co.

Charles H. Crump (1836–1917) joined Jones, Shreve, Brown & Co. in Boston in 1855. He helped reorganize the business and in 1869 became partner and general manager of what was now Shreve, Crump & Low. Charles, whose forebears on his mother's side came from Newport, Rhode Island, continued in the firm's tradition of adventurous Yankee merchants. At the time of his death in 1917, he had crossed the Atlantic Ocean eighty-eight times, and it was reported that one-half of his "business life had been spent in Europe."[1]

Foreign contacts were important to all major American firms, and Shreve, Crump & Low Co. had prospered from its European connections.

Jabez Gorham and the Founding of
The Gorham Company, Providence, Rhode Island

In the late eighteenth and early nineteenth centuries, the port of Providence was filled with small shops catering to the maritime trade, selling clocks, sextants, compasses, books, watches, and jewelry. Due to the miscellaneous nature of the merchandise, the terms novelty, notions, bric-a-brac and, in a derogatory sense, gewgaws (gaudy baubles) came into use to describe the early array of wares of these firms.

Another New England enterprise that began as a jewelry firm, which was later to be known as the Gorham Company, was established in Providence. In 1806 Jabez Gorham (1792–1869) was apprenticed to Nehemiah Dodge, the so-called Father of the Jewelry Industry in Rhode Island. The sign over his shop on Main Street in Providence read: "Goldsmith and Jeweler, Clock and Watch Maker."

Jabez Gorham started his first business with four other jewelers in 1813; it lasted until 1818, when the firm became simply "Jabez Gorham, Jeweler." This designation stood out among Providence's general stores.

The times had not been auspicious: the British had blockaded the eastern ports of the United States during the War of 1812–14, but such hindrances proved a spur to native industry. In 1820 Gorham moved his business to 12 Steeple Street, where he manufactured gold beads, earrings, breastpins, finger rings, and "French" filigree. There mere use of the word "French" increased the value and popularity of certain types of jewelry. Gorham's firm also made an article called the "Gorham chain." Since the creation of a recognizable style was greatly impeded at that time by the constant turnover in employees and the frequent changes in partnerships resulting from deaths, accidents, fires, and financial disruptions, the fact that one jeweler's gold chain could be singled out over another's was estimable.

Such wares as Jabez Gorham's—humble yet fashionable—were carried by Yankee pedlars all over the countryside, to Boston, New York, and Springfield. The success of these "drummers" in the field contributed to Gorham's ability to expand his operations. He was the first major manufacturer to wholesale gold and silver jewelry throughout America.

After a number of transformations in 1841, the original firm became J. Gorham & Son. This company manufactured spoons, buckles, thimbles, and other household items in silver. The sale of these utilitarian objects was more profitable than the jewelry sales. This changed the firm's direction from the original vision of its founder, Jabez Gorham—jeweler.

John Gorham

Jabez Gorham's son John (1820–98) was a man of his times: the power for his workshop came from a horse that pulled a shaft in the basement, but he had his heart set on a 50-horsepower steam engine. Installing the necessary new machinery in enlarged premises and taking on tenants to help defray expenses was a precarious undertaking for a small businessman. However, in doing so, John allied J. Gorham & Son with the Industrial Revolution in nineteenth-century America. He revolutionized the production of household silver by applying steam power, and the newest tool-and-die making and casting techniques. The firm's new-found ability to sell efficiently mass-produced silverware assured their recognition as fine silversmiths, a branch of the trade held to be distinct from jewelers at that time. J. Gorham & Son incorporated and became the Gorham Manufacturing Company in 1865.

Maiden Lane, New York City

Maiden Lane, *J. Maadji Paatji* in Dutch, was named after the Dutch dairymaids who drove their cows through the adjoining pastures and washed their laundry in the streams. After the American Revolution, the valley became commercial in character, with the arrival of dealers in steel, lead, and iron. It was not until the early 1800s that goldsmiths started to settle in Maiden Lane. It was then that New York's jewelry trade really began.

New York's jewelry industry started with jobbing houses and small wholesale establishments. These small entrepreneurs manufactured and sold their own wares, such as gold and silver thimbles, lockets, chains, and wedding rings. They also sold the wares made in Providence and in other New England towns. The pedlars who brought these wares to town sensed a good market and began to open their own retail shops.

As the number of jewelers on Maiden Lane increased during the early 1800s, their output became more imaginative. They sought to establish patronage among New York's small elite and a growing middle class who could afford a modest amount of jewelry. Filigree bow pins such as those by the New York filigree worker Joseph F. de Guerre remained popular into the eighties. Box pins, which had a compartment on either side to contain hair and a miniature, were also in demand. Gold mulberry earrings were so fashionable that the New York jeweler Joseph F. Chattellier, of Chattellier & Spencer at 625 Broadway, manufactured 1,800 successively.

In the 1890s, Lucy Benedict, one of America's first female journalists, while reporting on jewelry, summed up the work of this early period. "Large cameos were counted as the only parure for matrons; seed pearls mounted in *tumuli* [clusters of minuscule pearls] were the spoil of every bride: heavy pieces of blood red coral, with pendant grapes, the desire of every woman. Around his neck the butcher, the baker, the candlestick-maker and his female relations hung heavy gold chains, and the watering-place dandy of his day disported in a white duck suit and a chain-like halter. Bracelets were massive bands and rings weighty pieces of gold. What became of all these there is little need to ask. Every such period brings its own destruction."[2]

The Founding of Black, Starr & Frost, New York

When Erastus Barton founded his firm in 1810, Napoleon I and Britain were at war. Barton soon took a partner, Frederick Marquand, and Marquand & Barton was located at 166 Broadway, near Maiden Lane. Since virtually all trade during this period was carried to Europe in neutral American ships, fortunes were made along the east coast from shipping and related industries. Emigration was high too, and the population of New England's cities grew.

Like other American firms, Marquand & Barton lacked the family tradition of the Old World jewelry establishments, nor could it boast the patronage of an established aristocracy. These early American firms struggled to survive and went through many incorporations. Marquand & Barton experienced numerous changes of partners and associations: Marquand & Bros., Marquand & Co., Ball, Tompkins & Black (1839), and Ball, Black & Co. (1851).

The sequence of new partners was interspersed with changes in location. As jewelry businesses in New York prospered, they followed their growing clientele, migrating to the new fashionable areas of the city. This young New York firm exemplified this trend, moving to 181 Broadway in 1833 and to 247 Broadway in 1848. Soon a natural division, based on location, developed among jobbers, piece workers, wholesalers, and fine jewelry retailers.

The novelties sold by jewelers were constantly changing, of course. Ball, Tompkins & Black, for instance, sold the new kerosene lighting fixtures, which began to be popular in the 1850s. Along with these lamps, jewelers exhibited porcelain, silver, paintings, bronze statuettes, as well as jewelry.

4. Decorated Watches

Late 19th century
(clockwise from top left)

Watch, with an enamel miniature of a 19th-century painting by Pierre Auguste Cot, *Le Printemps*
Yellow gold, enamel, and half-pearls
Signed by Duhne Co., Cincinnati, Ohio

Watch, with a desert landscape and sphinx
Yellow gold, enamel, and diamonds
Signed and retailed by W.W. Wattles & Sons, Pittsburgh, Pennsylvania
Manufactured by Patek Philippe, Geneva

Pendant watch brooch with a floral design
Yellow gold, silver, enamel, and diamonds
Signed by Black, Starr & Frost

Pendant watch brooch, with a pattern of sea creatures and nymphs
Yellow gold
Signed by Theodore B. Starr

Watch, with an enamel miniature of the 19th-century painting by Gustave Courbet, *The Source*
Yellow gold, enamel, and diamonds
Signed by Waltham Watch Co.

Cortlandt W. Starr
Black, Starr & Frost

In the late 1860s following the Civil War, New York City's wealth equaled that of all the ex-Confederate states together. New York businessmen profited tremendously from the Civil War, supplying goods and services to the north. Some of the future leaders of the New York jewelry trade took advantage of the healthy economic climate to establish or to reorganize their firms.

During the Civil War, Cortlandt W. Starr (1833–88), one of the younger members of Ball, Black & Co., had maintained his own private military company; later he joined the 37th and the 71st Regiments, receiving the commission of second lieutenant. His military distinction proved to be an asset among New York's business and social elite. In 1874 Starr was elevated to partnership when Ball, Black & Co. reorganized. It became Black, Starr & Frost and moved farther Uptown to 251 Fifth Avenue in 1876. From this fashionable location, the firm met the new demand for small pieces of diamond jewelry. It produced and imported diminutive versions of reigning European styles—bows, flowers, leaves, and other ornaments.

Theodore B. Starr and Herman Marcus
Starr & Marcus, New York

Theodore B. Starr (1837–1907) came from a long line of Americans whose forebears included Dr. Comfort Starr, who had settled in Cambridge, Massachusetts, in 1635 and was one of the first overseers of Harvard College.

Theodore was born in New Rochelle, New York, in 1837 and entered the jewelry business as a messenger boy in 1853. He worked first for Reed, Taylor & Co. and later for Peckham, Merrill, Fitch & Co. at 19 John Street in New York City. Nine years later, he opened a small custom-order business at 18 John Street, and in 1864 Theodore Starr was successful enough to enter into partnership with Herman Marcus.

Herman Marcus (1828–99) was born in Germany on Christmas Day; he became an important figure in the New York jewelry trade. After finishing his education and joining Ellemeyer, the court jewelers of Dresden, where he acquired knowledge of the "mercantile side of the jewelry business,"[3] Marcus came to New York in 1850. There he worked successfully for Ball, Black & Co. and Tiffany & Co., before entering into the partnership with Starr. Their firm, Starr & Marcus, was a retail jewelry firm located on John Street. In the 1860s it was considered by the Gorham Company, the prestigious Providence silverware manufacturer, as a possible New York retail outlet for their work.

5. Sunburst Brooches with Pendant Attachments

Late 19th century

Opals, diamond, yellow gold, and platinum
Signed by Tiffany & Co.

Diamonds, yellow gold, and platinum
Signed by Theodore B. Starr

6. Necklace

Late 19th century

Moonstone cameo depicting the head of a bacchante, cultured pearls (contemporary), diamonds, rubies, platinum, and yellow gold
Signed Jaques & Marcus

7. Celtic Buckle

Early 20th century

Yellow gold, Mexican fire opal, emeralds, sapphires, and diamonds
Signed Theodore B. Starr

Starr & Marcus was part of the group of fine jewelers and silversmiths that included Tiffany & Co., the Whiting Manufacturing Co., the Gorham Company, and Black, Starr & Frost. These five firms were asked to submit final designs for a vase to be made in 1875 in honor of the Transcendentalist poet William Cullen Bryant. The competition was sponsored by J. P. Morgan, Theodore Roosevelt, and other prominent Americans. The finished object was to be displayed at the Centennial Exposition held in Philadelphia the following year, a significant honor.

Although Tiffany & Co. won the competition, Starr & Marcus produced a notable display for the 1876 Centennial Exposition. It included diamond and pink oriental pearl necklaces, a diamond aigrette, coral brooches, and a collection of rare cameos and intaglios, some set in cloisonné-enamel mounts.

Philadelphia Firms

In the 1830s James Emmett Caldwell (1813–81) and his partner, a Mr. Bennett, founded a watch, clock and jewelry establishment in Philadelphia, which had been the nation's capital until 1788 and was still one of the most prosperous cities in the eastern United States.

Caldwell was born in Poughkeepsie, New York, and had apprenticed to P. P. Hayes, a silversmith in Philadelphia. Caldwell then worked a short time in New York, on Maiden Lane, before setting up in business in Philadelphia.

Caldwell's and Bennett's small establishment underwent many changes of partners and addresses; in 1868 it became J. E. Caldwell Co. at 822 Chestnut Street. That same year, after a serious fire, the partners rebuilt in an improved location at 902 Chestnut Street. In 1916, the firm moved to the corner of Juniper and Chestnut Streets in Philadelphia's wealthiest shopping district.

In 1832 another jewelry business, Joseph Trowbridge Bailey with his partner Andrew B. Kitchen, set up on Chestnut Street. Bailey & Kitchen were manufacturing and retailing jewelers; they specialized in silverware, jewelry, and other articles. In 1846, Joseph's brother E. W. Bailey (of Maiden Lane, New York) joined the firm, which, with two additional partners, became Bailey & Co.

In 1878, George Banks of J. E. Caldwell & Co. and Samuel Biddle of Robbins, Clark & Biddle joined Joseph T. Bailey II of Bailey & Co. to form Bailey, Banks & Biddle.

It was located at Twelfth and Chestnut Streets. By this time, this firm and the other successful Philadelphia jewelers were emulating the popular New York styles. The fashionable floral ornaments were now further enhanced by the use of colorful semiprecious stones—topazes, moonstones, and tourmalines.

Southern Jewelers

Two firms of jewelers from the south, Samuel Kirk & Son Co. of Baltimore and Galt & Bros. of Washington, D.C., were founded in the early days of the American republic and supplied valuable articles to its political and military figures. Samuel Kirk made gifts for George Washington and was commissioned by the city of Baltimore to make two silver cups for General Lafayette when he visited the city in the early nineteenth century.

Kirk, a Quaker from Doylestown, Pennsylvania, and a descendant of English silversmiths, came to Baltimore in 1815 and opened a small shop on Market Street. (In 1814, Maryland had enacted the first law concerning the stamping of silver in America.) The assay marks of the early Kirk pieces date from this period.

Galt & Bros. in Washington, D.C., which was situated in a town that was little more than a government outpost at the time, was founded during Thomas Jefferson's presidency. The firm's signed objects included pistols, swords, and presentation medals, as well as silverware and gold and silver jewelry.

Greenleaf & Crosby, Jacksonville, Florida

Jacksonville, Florida, was one of the most important southern ports after the Civil War. Greenleaf & Crosby was established there, on 9 West Bay Street, in 1867. The firm's partners, Damon Greenleaf and J. H. Crosby, Jr., came from Rockford, Illinois, and North Adams, Massachusetts, respectively. Crosby was a "practical jeweler"[4] who had learned his trade in Vermont. Similar to the offerings of eastern jewelry establishments of an earlier period, Greenleaf & Crosby's merchandise was specific to the region and tastes of its partners: jewelry, Florida souvenirs, and a collection of rare live tropical birds and wild animals. The last department came under the jurisdiction of Greenleaf, who was also president of the Florida State Park Association.

As the tourist trade in Florida developed, branches of Greenleaf & Crosby sprang up near the luxury hotels Henry Flagler built along the coast. Branches were opened in the Alcazar, St. Augustine, in 1887; in the Royal Poinciana Hotel, Palm Beach, in 1895; and later in the Breakers and the Royal Hotel of Downtown Miami at the turn of the century. By the 1920s the firm had become the foremost jeweler both to Florida residents and to the entrepreneurs who were making these southern communities famous as resorts.

Midwestern Jewelers

The Jaccard and Mermod Families, St. Louis, Missouri

The watchmaker Louis Jaccard came to St. Louis from Switzerland in 1829. The business he opened in a shop with one door and a window on Main Street was the first of its type in the Mississippi region. A relative, A. S. Mermod, joined the business in 1845. By the latter part of the nineteenth century, the firm and its many offshoots started by other family members were the best-known jewelers west of the Mississippi. They profited from St. Louis's advantageous location, serving as the gateway to the West and as a major center of the flourishing Mississippi River trade. These firms augmented their own wares—primarily watches and sentimental jewelry—with inventory imported from the northeast.

The Founding of C. D. Peacock, Chicago, Illinois

In contrast to the eastern cities, Chicago was still a frontier town. In 1837 Elijah Peacock, a third-generation English silver- and goldsmith, set up a small jewelry store with a 10 × 20 foot workroom, where he employed his young son Charles (1838–1903). This establishment produced and sold clocks and watches, supplemented by the usual line of small jewelry of the period—gold and silver chains, lockets, wedding rings, and the like. Charles looked after the fires, tinkered with the watches and cleaned them, and delivered goods to the pioneer settlers. Later the young man would give his name to the firm and move it from its early location on Lake Street to the corner of Randolph and Franklin Streets. That shop was destroyed by the great Chicago Fire of 1871. Elijah Peacock then went into real estate and urban redevelopment, leaving the prominent jewelry firm to his son, who developed it further. After the fire, the firm moved to 96 West Madison Street, then to Washington Street, and finally to 101 South State Street, the prestigious address where it is today.

Spaulding & Co., Chicago, Illinois

By the third quarter of the nineteenth century, the enthusiasm in America for fine jewelry had become infectious. This strengthened the old jewelry firms and inspired new ones.

On January 1, 1889, H. A. Spaulding & Co. opened in Chicago. Spaulding came from C. L. Tiffany's Paris branch—a notable qualification. His new Chicago firm started to produce the finest diamond jewelry in the West—hair ornaments, necklaces, brooches, and rings.

The Gorham Company also played an integral part in Spaulding & Co.'s career. A Gorham executive purchased for Spaulding & Co. the lease, fixtures, and inventory of a well-situated Chicago jewelry firm that had recently gone bankrupt. The agreement included Spaulding & Co.'s guaranteeing a prestigious retail outlet in Chicago for the Gorham Company. The two firms continued to be closely associated for the next fifty years.

Spaulding had profited from his time in Paris. In 1881 and 1882 he had traveled to all the courts of Europe, where he had met with various heads of state and dignitaries. The Crystal Palace Exhibition in London and subsequent Paris expositions made such an impression on him that he conceived the idea of The Museum of Living History for the upper West Side of New York City, "which will be for the United States even more than what the Kensington Museum is for England, for it is hoped that it will become the Parthenon of America."[5] The scheme was of such gigantic proportions, that it never materialized. Even the most prominent magazine of the trade, *The Jewelers' Circular and Horological Review*, demurred when faced with the task of describing it.

Gump's, San Francisco, California

In 1861, Solomon Gump inherited his brother-in-law's frame and mirror shop in San Francisco. It was a thriving enterprise, for mirrors were continually being broken in rowdy saloons and hotels in the early days of the Gold Rush. With his profits from this business, Gump went to Europe and bought paintings and sculpture; then he sold them to those participants in the Gold Rush who moved from camps to mansions. Later Solomon's son A. L. Gump traveled to the Orient, where he purchased oriental objets d'art: screens, porcelain, jade beads, and stones. While Shreve & Co. supplied San Francisco with European-style jewelry from the East Coast, Gump's became famous for oriental exotica and jade jewelry.

The American Jeweler

By 1876, America's first centennial, the jewelry trade had come into its own as a unique industry. *The Jewelers' Circular and Horological Review* was one of the earliest American journal devoted exclusively to the craft and was first published in 1874 in New York City. It soon reported news from jewelers and tradesmen throughout the quickly growing young country. The thriving mercantile atmosphere of post-Civil War America overshadowed the staunch frugality of the early colonists.

As Americans became willing to spend more money and interested in other jewelry besides trinkets of a sentimental nature, the trade in precious jewelry became more profitable. However, the use of precious stones and finer gold and silver demanded a greater capital output. The shopkeepers and artisans who went on to become fine jewelers were those who could raise the capital and reinvest their profits in increasingly expensive—and desirable items.

By always turning a profit, however small, these merchants and craftsmen positioned themselves to make fortunes when the American economy began the rapid growth that lasted through the late nineteenth century. Men like Shreve, Caldwell, Spaulding, and Tiffany, among others, seized the spirit of the time and went on to become great merchants.

Chapter Two

The Establishment of Tiffany & Co.

Charles Lewis Tiffany

Charles Lewis Tiffany (1812–1902) was the son of a New England mill owner and retailer. At fifteen, he assumed management of his father's newly opened store in Danielsonville, Connecticut.

New England, in the nineteenth century, was famous for its water-driven workshops, the output of which was exhibited as "Yankee notions" and praised at the Crystal Palace Exhibition in London in 1851. The region was an important industrial area, with New York City as its financial center; the Erie Canal (completed in 1825) provided a conduit for New England's goods on their way to Ohio, Indiana, and further west.

Tiffany & Young / Tiffany, Young & Ellis

In September, 1837, Charles Tiffany and his friend John B. Young went into business together in New York City. They founded Tiffany & Young at 259 Broadway.

Tiffany was a man with financial acumen as well as great personal charm. Businesses were feeling the strain of the Panic of 1837, which was the worst financial crisis the United States had known to date. Tiffany's formula for success consisted of selling bric-a-brac—fashionable decorative objects for the home. From the outset, his goods were of a finer quality than any other New York store's. In order to do this, he befriended sea captains just in from the Orient, going to the docks personally and choosing the best goods at first hand. Tiffany's judgment proved to be unerring; the merchandise sold well. When the hard times subsided, the ensuing financial recovery brought an increased demand for luxury goods; New England's jewelry manufacturers were unable to meet the demand alone. Not what to stock, but where to find merchandise became the urgent question. The answer revolved around another New England enterprise—shipping. The American merchant marine, one of the best in the world, was now able to provide a safe and relatively inexpensive passage to Europe.

8. Cameo Brooches
19th century
Signed by Tiffany & Co.
(top to bottom)

Brooch with pendant attachment
Rectangular agate cameo depicting
the Triumph of Aphrodite.
Diamonds and yellow gold

Brooch with pendant attachment
With inscribed date "Apr. 30, 1884"
Oval agate cameo on a pink ground,
with a pastoral scene.
Diamonds and yellow gold

Rectangular agate cameo depicting
the revels of eroti.
Diamonds and yellow gold

In 1841, the addition of a new partner, J. L. Ellis, enabled the firm to take advantage of this situation and investigate foreign sources of supply. Tiffany stayed in New York with Ellis; Young was elected to go to Europe, armed with letters of introduction, reference, and credit.

Young's mission became an educational process, one that would determine the future course of the business. On this trip, he acquired Tiffany's first collection of jewelry —gaudy, inexpensive costume jewelry from Hanau, Germany, which was all they could afford at the time. Though crude and heavy, these pieces proved so popular that, on the next buying trip, the firm was able to purchase a finer, more delicate line of paste from Paris, named Palais Royal. This was an even greater success, indicative of the growing American market for jewelry.

The firm's increasing capital and reputation enabled it to invest in fine jewelry at last. It imported real gold and diamond jewelry from workshops in Paris and London. The rate of turnover for these pieces was so high that they could not be obtained fast enough nor in sufficient quantity to meet the demand. Therefore, in 1848, the firm began to create its own gold and diamond jewelry and to scour Europe for diamonds. The most obvious source was the late eighteenth-century diamond jewelry that belonged to Europe's aristocracy and was becoming easier to obtain.

Tiffany, Reed & Co., Paris

In France, the July Monarchy of Louis Philippe was overthrown during the February Revolution of 1848, and the citizen king and his consort, Marie Amelie, fled for their lives, as did members of their court. There was unrest throughout Europe in this period. Jewelry was changing hands rapidly, and in those days of turmoil, diamonds fell 50 percent in value.

The American firm of Tiffany, Young & Ellis put its assets to work, acquiring the noted "girdle of Marie Antoinette." Shortly afterward, it set up a Paris branch to manage such spontaneous transactions more expeditiously; this branch was under the direction of a new partner, Gideon F. T. Reed (1817–92). Reed had been prominent in the Boston jewelry trade and had owned his own firm, Lincoln, Reed & Co.

Tiffany, Reed & Co., as the new Parisian branch was called, had a succession of offices: at 79 Rue Richelieu, at 57 Rue de Chateaud'un, and at Avenue de l'Opéra 36 Bis. Founded in 1850, the year of Napoleon III's coup d'état, Tiffany, Reed & Co. grew up with the Second Empire. With a unique diamond-oriented inventory, the Parisian branch of the American firm was soon purveying fine jewelry on two continents.

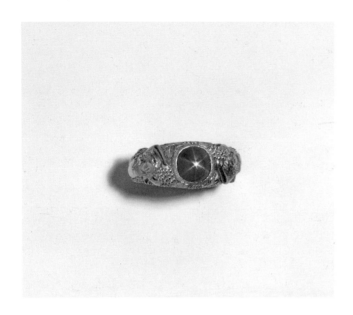

9. Gentleman's Ring
Late 19th century

Yellow gold with a pattern of
bacchantes and grapes, and a star
sapphire
Signed by Tiffany & Co.

10. Watch Bracelet
20th century

Painted enamel medallions depicting
female figures from mythology
Yellow gold, enamel, diamonds, and
emeralds
Signed Tiffany & Co.

Panel Bracelet
19th century

Sculpted goldwork depicting reclining
female figures with roses and doves
Yellow gold, enamel, and diamonds in
platinum mounts
Signed by the French jeweler Joë
Descomps
In a fitted case signed Tiffany & Co.,
221 Regent St., London W

American Silver and John C. Moore

In addition to fine gold and diamond jewelry, Tiffany, Young & Ellis had been importing English household silverware. In 1851 with prohibitive American tariffs being placed on imported foreign goods, Charles Tiffany managed to circumvent the situation. He arranged an agreement with John C. Moore and his son Edward, the finest silverware manufacturers in New York, to produce work exclusively for Tiffany, Young & Ellis and its Paris branch.

At this time, silverware was the most important status item in America. Elegant silver place settings, tea sets, trays, as well as commemorative trophies, boxes, and christening sets were the harbingers of America's growing desire for luxury. Moore had previously been supplying Tiffany's main competitors: the Gorham Company, Marquand & Co., and their successors, Ball, Tompkins & Black. Moore's move to Tiffany established the firm's preeminence. The profits from his work helped provide the capital for Tiffany's entry into the finer jewelry markets of the world.

Tiffany, Young & Ellis was the first American firm to adopt the English standard of sterling silver (925/1000), anticipating by about fifteen years a similar move by the Gorham Company and the rest of the industry. In so doing, the Tiffany firm separated itself from other American firms whose silverware was substandard. The logic of standardizing this early should be put in the context of the desirability of world markets: the firm of Tiffany was determined to sell on a grand and magnificent scale to Europeans. Later, with the discovery of silver in Colorado and of the Comstock Lode in Nevada in 1859, silver from sources native to the United States would satisfy all demand abundantly. Tiffany, Young & Ellis's early contributions to the development of the silverware industry led to the firm's unprecedented success in foreign markets and was the source of tremendous revenues.

In 1853, Charles Tiffany's partners Young and Ellis retired. The firm, which became Tiffany & Co. at that date, moved to a new, fashionable location at 550 Broadway.

Tiffany & Co. and the Civil War

New York jewelry firms began to be involved in wartime activities with the Civil War. They adapted their stock, in a somewhat surprising manner, to the new demands. Ball, Black & Co. (now situated at 565 Broadway) advertised in 1861 in the *New York Daily*

11. Flower Brooch
19th century

Yellow gold, Montana sapphires, and rubies
Signed by Tiffany & Co.

12. Lace and Bonnet Pins
19th century
Signed by Tiffany & Co.
(clockwise from top left)

Bonnet
Diamonds, demantoid garnets, yellow gold, and platinum
Shown at the World's Columbian Exposition in Chicago, 1893

Bee
Grey pearl, diamonds, rubies, and yellow gold

Horseshoe
Brooch with pendant attachment
Diamond, rubies, and yellow gold

Tribune that it sold: "camp chest and Ball's American Camp Cooking Range and Boiler to officers of Army and Navy . . . Cooking Range and Boiler made of the best Russian iron and very durable . . . indispensable articles . . . conducive to their health and comfort in the camp."[1]

Tiffany & Co. enlarged its premises and profited tremendously by transforming the adjoining building at 552 Broadway into a military depot containing merchandise to be shipped to all parts of the "Loyal States."[2] This comprehensive array included "Swords warranted to cut wrought iron . . . Cap Ornaments and other Embroideries from Paris. Gold epaulettes and Navy Laces, etc., from London."[3] In addition, there were more predictable supplies: medals and twenty thousand badges for the state of Ohio, and everyday items like caps, rifles, ambulances, and army shoes.

The northern states outshone the southern states in the production of military paraphernalia. Accordingly, the war-related industries in the north prospered in the early 1860s, making fortunes instead of experiencing a depression. "Armour (meat packing), Havemeyer (sugar), Weyerhaeuser (lumber), Huntington (merchandise and railroads), Remington (guns), Rockefeller (oil), Carnegie (iron and steel), Borden (milk), and Marshall Field (merchandise)"[4] became household words in the period following Reconstruction, and for decades to come were identified with their goods and products. This was also the case for Tiffany & Co. The profits earned during the war years catapulted Tiffany into the rank of these other great American businesses. However, unlike the aforementioned companies, Tiffany & Co. returned to its prewar endeavors, producing silverware and acquiring fine jewelry.

The Incorporation of Tiffany & Co.

Tiffany & Co. incorporated in 1868, with Charles Lewis Tiffany as president and treasurer, Gideon F. T. Reed of the Paris branch as vice-president, Charles T. Cook as general superintendent and assistant treasurer, and George McClure as secretary. Under their management, the firm was unrivaled in America. It owned an enlarged plant in New York, a Paris branch, a new London branch (at 29 Argyll Street), and an office and watch manufactory at 7 Rue Leverrier in Geneva. (The Geneva office operated only a short time, for the firm found it more advantageous to delegate its patents and designs to a Swiss enterprise for production.) Until 1880, Tiffany & Co. was the sole distributor of Patek Philippe & Co. of Geneva in this country, a further indication of their foreign affiliations. They represented that famous Swiss firm at the Centennial Exposition of 1876 in Philadelphia.

On November 10, 1870, Tiffany & Co. moved to the corner of Union Square and Fifteenth Street, a site previously occupied by the Church of the Puritans. The firm erected a fireproof building—one of the first in New York—with a cast-iron exterior and burglar-proof vaults in the basement. The first three floors were reserved for silverware, diamonds, jewelry, watches, fancy goods, leather goods, umbrellas, fans, stationery, plated ware, statuary, bric-a-brac, clocks, mantel sets, lamps, curios, reproductions of ancient armor, and other ornamental objects for the home. Almost anything of this kind that was available in Europe could now be had at Tiffany & Co. in America.

The fourth floor was set aside for special exhibits. The fifth floor contained a large workshop for diamond cutting, polishing, and the fabrication of leather jewelry cases.

In addition to offices, situated throughout the building, there were facilities for making repairs to watches and jewelry.

The firm was a full-fledged manufacturing company. The director in charge of production was the silversmith Edward C. Moore. He was in charge of the silverworks at Prince Street, a small plated-ware workshop in Newark, New Jersey, and later the 7-acre plant in Forest Hill, New Jersey.

#23 Bicolor
Cutlega
Brazil

THIS DRAWING TO BE
RETURNED TO
TIFFANY & CO.
WHO RESERVE THE SOLE
RIGHT TO ESTIMATE
UPON IT.

#23

Chapter Three

Tiffany & Co. and the International Expositions, 1867–1900

The Importance of the International Expositions

In the second half of the nineteenth century, the successive international expositions—often termed World's Fairs—gave the United States an opportunity to establish a national identity in an international arena. The excellence of one country in any field at these expositions had a great influence on its sales. At the 1867 Exposition in Paris, Tiffany & Co. won the first prize ever awarded by an international jury to the United States for its exhibit of silver tableware—"a display of the plainer patterns of domestic plates."[1] The entries of other American jewelers at the Centennial Exposition in Philadelphia in 1876 were even more impressive.

Surprises at the Centennial Exposition in Philadelphia (1876)

13. Orchid Brooch Study and Photograph
1889
Signed by Tiffany & Co.

A page depicting number twenty-three of the twenty-five orchid brooches shown at the 1889 Exposition, Paris
Enamel and yellow gold, with gem-set stem
From the Tiffany & Co. scrapbook, *Paris [Exposition] 1889*

The Swiss commission at the Centennial Exposition was astonished by the accuracy of America's mass-produced timepieces, particularly those made by the Waltham and Elgin companies. The quality of American watches had overtaken Europe's during the Civil War, when every soldier had wanted his own watch. This had created a boom in the industry. Since there were no American watch entries at the 1862 Exposition in Paris and since the Tiffany & Co. watch display at the 1867 Exposition had been modest, the Swiss had underestimated what was happening in American factories. Instead of exporting good watches to the United States, they had been sending the "worst trash"[2] and the effect had been beneficial to American watchmakers.

During the Civil War, American watchmakers had enlarged their factories and set their sights on a "better, ordinary watch."[3] The formula for their success was summed up in the Swiss report, "Their tools work so regularly, that all parts of the watches may be interchanged by a simple order on a postal card."[4]

By now, technological advances were affecting the production of both silverware and watches. Water and steam power, accuracy in measuring and in machining tools and dies, and an emphasis on the standardization of parts were the heritage of Yankee tinkerers and small businessmen.

Two years later, at the 1878 Exposition in Paris, a Massachusetts watchmaking firm, Waltham, received the gold medal, the highest award given to any exhibiter in horology.

In 1854, *Putnam's Magazine* had published the following statement, which proved prophetic, "The genius of this new country is necessarily mechanical. Our greatest thinkers are not in the library, nor the capitol, but in the machine shop. The American people is intent on studying, not the hieroglyphic monuments of ancient genius, but how best to subdue and till the soil of its boundless territories, how to build roads and ships, and how to apply the powers of nature to the work of manufacturing its rich materials into forms of utility and enjoyment. The youth of this country are learning the sciences not as theories, but with reference to their application to the arts. Our education is no genial culture of letters, but simply learning the use of tools."[5]

Nineteenth-Century Technology: Jewelry

Although watchmaking, silversmithing, and goldsmithing were considered allied trades, very little of the new technology was affecting the production of fine jewelry. Mechanization had been applied chiefly to less expensive trinkets, which were mass-produced. The prevailing idea was that soon no one in the United States would be too poor to own, at least, a ring and a brooch. At the Centennial Exposition, equal coverage was given to the Tiffany & Co. display of the so-called Brunswick canary diamond and to the ornaments nearby made of a new substance—celluloid. In jewelry at this time, the appeal of the intrinsic value of a piece had, in general, not yet overtaken the appeal of technological novelty.

The Roman jeweler Alessandro Castellani was a featured speaker at the Centennial Exposition. His jewelry in the Etruscan style had caused a sensation at the 1862 Exposition in Paris, which had taken place during America's Civil War and was unattended by American jewelers. Now, in 1876, Castellani was describing to them the revival jewelry made famous by his family firm and explaining his experiments with ancient goldsmithing techniques.

As a result of his enthusiastic presentation, amphoras and other classical elements were incorporated into American gold jewelry, lockets, chains, brooches, and bracelets. Unlike Castellani's magnificent productions, the American versions were plainer and less expensive. The majority were mass produced and did not incorporate gems. In the technical coverage of the period, the term "Etruscan finish" was applied to a matte gold finish.

One year after the exposition, Tiffany & Co. contributed to the archeological style with replicas of gold jewelry from a collection of Cypriote antiquities assembled by General Louis Palma di Cesnola, the former American Consul to Cyprus, who became director of the Metropolitan Museum of Art that year.

The 1878 Exposition in Paris

The year following the Centennial Exposition, the partnership of Starr & Marcus dissolved. Herman Marcus returned to Tiffany & Co. and represented them at the 1878 Exposition in Paris, where the firm won the Grand Prix for silverware, a gold medal for jewelry for the display of the Cesnola Collection, and six additional medals.

Charles Tiffany appeared in person at the exposition and received the highest honor: he was awarded the rank of Chevalier in France's Legion of Honor; appointed, as gold- and silversmith, Imperial or Royal Jeweler to most of the courts of Europe; and received a Gold Medal *Praemia Digno* from the emperor of Russia.

Another Display of Technological Ability

The Tiffany & Co. display at the Paris exposition was notable for its silver pitchers, vases, creamers and other containers in the style of the mixed metalware of Japan, which members of the firm had seen two years earlier at the Centennial Exposition. They had been profoundly influenced by the Japanese craftsmanship; and one Japanese artisan, Karasawa Takaota, had actually worked with American silversmiths at the Tiffany silver workshops.

The idea of using mixed metals to achieve color was new and exciting; it inspired America's craftsmen. To remove areas of metal, American craftsmen employed acid etching rather than using the cold-chiseling techniques utilized by the Japanese. In many cases the Americans soldered in the inlays (usually made of copper alloys), finishing the object afterward with engraving and chasing. They also experimented with color patination, lacquer, and simple opaque enamels. The total effect of such pieces was astonishing to Europeans and Americans alike. No one had expected such technological innovations from the New World's metalsmiths. They applied these techniques to small pieces of jewelry, in particular cravat pins, pendants, brooches, and perfume vials.

Tiffany & Co. had not been above taking risks: the success of their gamble created an atmosphere of anticipation—which continued into the twentieth century—around their exhibits at the international expositions.

Tiffany & Co.'s Purchase of the French Crown Jewels (1887)

Americans have always been fascinated by Europe's crown jewels. In 1881, *The Jewelers' Circular and Horological Review* reported, "It is a well-known fact that this country absorbs more diamonds than any other and that the finest gems that come from the hands of the lapidaries are in greatest demand here. The demand, in fact, for rare gems is so great that it cannot be supplied and fabulous prices are being paid for them. Many wealthy persons regard diamonds as the best class of securities in which they invest their money; they pay no interest certainly, but neither do they suffer from depreciation."[6]

American gem buyers followed the fortunes of Empress Eugenie's collection of diamond jewelry, which was rumored to be coming on the market. The government of France at that time did not consider these jewels truly historical, since Empress Eugenie had had the diamond ornaments of previous monarchs redone by her own court jewelers. Her jewelry collection evoked the recently deposed Napoleonic court and that of Marie Antoinette, neither of which were very popular with the French at the time. Americans were dazzled by both—but chiefly by the diamonds themselves.

The French government considered organizing a raffle of these jewels, with chances selling at prices ranging from 5 to 25 dollars (the exchange rate of the day). They expected something like a hundred million dollars worth to be sold—this event was world news. Later, however, the idea was discarded.

Then, in 1887, the sale of the French crown jewels finally became a reality. They had been exhibited at the 1878 Exposition in Paris and again in the Louvre in 1884. An album of photographs was prepared by the French government in advance of the sale and presented to a few New York jewelers. At the time, *The Jewelers' Circular and Horological Review* reported discreetly, ". . . they were, as is well-known, mostly

Empress Eugenie's diamond jewelry

Late 19th-century photograph
A page from *Diamants de la couronne de France*, Photographie Berthaud, 9 Rue Cadet, Paris

purchased by dealers."[7] Tiffany & Co. had bought twenty-four lots, over one-third of the collection, for $500,000. It was the largest, single purchase of the entire sale and the most publicized investment the firm made in crown jewels in the nineteenth century.

In the final act of this dramatic sale, many of the jewels disappeared from public view to surface later in America. In 1899, *The Jewelers' Circular and Horological Review* discussed the Vanderbilt family's jewels, adding, "The collection includes most of the gems with which the Empress Eugenie once dazzled Paris."[8] Among them were several diamond and pearl tiaras, elaborate diamond brooches, hair ornaments, and seven unmounted historic diamonds. When Consuelo Vanderbilt married the Duke of Marlborough in 1895, her mother gave her two strings of pearls: one had belonged to Catherine the Great, and the other to Empress Eugenie.

The 1889 Exposition in Paris

The publicity surrounding Empress Eugenie's collection of jewelry had been steady for a decade. Furthermore, diamonds had been discovered in South Africa, and the plentiful supply served to make the public more diamond-oriented than ever before. In 1879 Tiffany & Co. acquired a 287.42 carat rough diamond from the early Kimberley mining operation in South Africa and had it cut in Paris. This was the Tiffany Diamond, the largest, flawless yellow diamond ever found. Seven years later Tiffany & Co. created the famous Tiffany setting, a six-prong setting that held a single diamond. It was an immediate success and "the Tiffany setting" was soon America's most popular engagement ring.

The more adventurous jewelers tired of the all-diamond jewelry styles that continued through the 1880s and of the restrictions imposed by this fashion for a single stone—they wanted color.

Tiffany & Co., moved by the vastness of the natural resources and mineral wealth of the United States, responded in a most flamboyant and unexpected way—they introduced a collection of jewels with native American themes and gems.

The theme was clear: "The striking feature in the collection that will constitute Tiffany & Co.'s display at the forthcoming Paris Exposition, leaving aside its magnitude, value, and beauty, resides in its being of thoroughly American character. Not only did the artisans whose hands wrought these beautiful objects receive their training in the Tiffany shops, but the designs of the principal part of the collection are of pure American character, being a refinement to the point of perfection of the graceful and quaint forms which have been unearthed among the rude implements made by the native American Indians."[9] Tiffany & Co. was awarded a gold medal in jewelry for this exhibit.

The publicity in France and at home was immense. The designs themselves came as a surprise to the entire viewing audience, because nothing resembling them appeared elsewhere. The first three brooches on the official list were indicative of the whole collection. The shapes were taken from "the carved wooden masks used by the medicine men of the Chillkat Indians, Alaska," the basketwork of the Hupa Indians, and "the decorated horse-hide shields used in warfare by the Sioux Indians."[10] This part of American culture was disappearing quickly, and like other American artists and ethnographers, Tiffany & Co. was responding in its own way.

The basis for this brilliant idea for a jewelry collection was rooted in archaeology and anthropology and in the almost reverent feeling American settlers held for their adopted land. Tiffany & Co.'s descriptions of the materials used in the jewels—brown pearls from Tennessee, sapphires from Montana, garnets from Arizona, fossil coral from Iowa, smoky rock crystal from Colorado, and opal agate from Mexico—were as evocative of the West and the frontier as were the paintings of Frederic Remington (1861–1909).

Even the jewel cases were made from American woods: California redwood, Alaska cypress, maple, and cherry. Their leather coverings were of black panther, coon, lizard, alligator, and chameleon—all New World species—and the linings of elkskin, ooze calfskin, and reindeerskin.

In the history of eye-catching international exhibitions, the 1889 presentation of Tiffany & Co. must have been one of the most provocative. The theme, which was carried out in the most minute detail, was a challenge to anyone daring to follow—but no one did.

George Frederick Kunz

The late nineteenth century was a period of expeditions, each one providing fresh information and exciting interest all over the world in the resources and history of the New World.

Tiffany & Co.'s gem expert, George Frederick Kunz, was a scientist with a breadth of knowledge in his field comparable to that of the well-known American geologist Clarence King, author of the classic book *Mountaineering in the Sierra Nevadas*, or of Ferdinand Vanderveer Hayden, who surveyed Yellowstone and invited Thomas Moran to be his guest artist.

Diamond corsage ornament

Photograph from the Tiffany & Co. Scrapbook, *Paris [Exposition] 1889*

Kunz went to Tiffany & Co. in 1879. From 1883 to 1909, he was a special member of the U.S. Geological Survey, and he served on the U.S. Fish Commission from 1892 to 1898, studying American pearls and investigating all the information that might prove pertinent to the firm. Kunz later wrote a series of outstanding texts: *Gems of North America* (1890), *The Book of the Pearl* (1908), *The Curious Lore of Precious Stones* (1913), *The Magic of Jewels* (1915), and *Rings* (1917).

At the 1889 Exposition in Paris, Kunz displayed a large collection of unmounted American gems and rare mineral specimens against the backdrop of the American jewelry exhibit. He included not only the familiar gemstones—sapphire, ruby, emerald and others—but also "a number of rare stones probably cut for the first time for jewelers' use, i.e. pectolite [blue], wollastonite [white], samarskite [black], dumortierite [blue and other colors], beryllonite [colorless], etc. Some of these specimens were kindly loaned by leading collectors, while others are the result of several years of careful search for this purpose by Tiffany & Co., George F. Kunz, their expert, having made special visits to some localities to obtain specimens."[11] He won a gold medal for his display of ornamental stones.

Kunz also included a collection of American fresh-water pearls in that exhibit, which were shown with their shells. These pearls came from the Little Miami in Ohio and other American rivers which produced more than half of the total American supply, valued at about a quarter of a million dollars at that time. The pearl collection had been acquired by Tiffany & Co. from I. Harris of Wayneville, Ohio, who had spent twenty years assembling it. The sources were now exhausted through indiscriminate harvesting and industrial pollution.

Tiffany & Co.'s collection of gems and pearls exhibited at the 1889 Exposition was so comprehensive that the twenty-year-old American Museum of Natural History in New York requested that it be kept intact and donated to the museum for study purposes. (J. P. Morgan supplied the funds for this gift.)

Kunz continued to collect under the auspices of Tiffany & Co., adding mineralogical specimens from all over the world to what became the museum's Morgan-Tiffany Collection of Gems. A variety of pink spodumene, found in California, was named kunzite after him in recognition of his efforts in this field.

American Enamels: The Tiffany & Co. Orchids

Tiffany & Co. had another extraordinary display at the 1889 Exposition, a collection of twenty-five enamel orchids. That year *The Jewelers' Circular and Horological Review* reported enthusiastically, "Among the enamel flower work are many beautiful

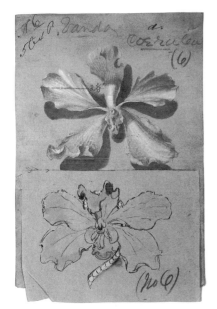

Tiffany orchid

A page with a watercolor rendering, sketch and photograph of one of the twenty-five three-dimensional orchid brooches in enamel from the Tiffany & Co. Scrapbook, *Paris [Exposition] 1889*

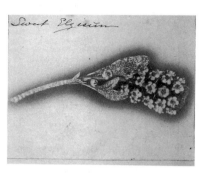

Four Tiffany flowers

A page with photographs of one wildflower and three orchid brooches from the Tiffany & Co. Scrapbook, *Paris [Exposition] 1889*

specimens in breast pins, brooches, earrings, and vinaigrettes of entirely original design, and of superior class of workmanship to that ever done in this country."[12]

A group of twenty-five three-dimensional orchids were singled out for comment and praise. The blossoms were accurately rendered in gold and painted enamel; some had diamond centers and gem-set stems. A few of the varieties were listed: among them, "the *Cattleya* bi-color and the *Odontoglossum zygopetalum* of the Brazils, the *Oncidium tigrinum*, the *Oncidium ornithorynchum* and the *Odontoglossum maculatum* of Mexico; the *Odontoglossum alexandrae* and the *Odontoglossum harryanum* of Colombia."[13]

These enameled orchids were remarkable creations that generated interest and admiration in Paris, particularly in the city's jewelry-making community. They were remembered long after the exhibition. *The Jewelers' Circular and Horological Review* reported in 1927, ". . . French bijoutiers [*sic.*] did not hesitate to acknowledge that in certain details of their craft they owed a debt to their Transatlantic brethren, and visited the American section in great numbers, not merely to gratify their curiosity, but for purposes of study."[14]

The exhibit of these flowers provided an additional incentive for the great revival in enameling that took place in Europe during the last decade of the nineteenth century.

A recurrent theme in the development of American jewelry was the growing chauvinism of jewelry craftsmen in the United States. Tiffany & Co. was quick to stress that only Americans had worked on their American jewelry collection for the 1889 Exposition. This created a problem for the firm's rival in the silverware trade—the Gorham Company—it was forced to admit at home and abroad (publicly and apologetically) that artisans from England, France, Russia, Germany, and other countries, as well as from America, had contributed to its display.

American wits did not fail to take note of Tiffany & Co.'s growing success and international stature. According to Gath, an American satirist of the 1890s, the original shop had sold stationery and gewgaws. The search for fine, international goods then yielded "pinchbeck, mere brilliants, and fixed-up things."[15] Later, he said, "The Americans intimated that they would like to have something genuine"[16] and so, in essence, still according to Gath, Tiffany's began to buy crown jewels.

World's Columbian Exposition in Chicago (1893)

The Tiffany & Co. exhibit at the World's Columbian Exposition of 1893 was impressive. The firm continued to work with multicolored gems—pink topazes, yellow sapphires, tourmalines, demantoid garnets, and aquamarines—in an eclectic American style that

14. Flower Jewels

1880s
Signed by Tiffany & Co.
(clockwise from top left)

Wildflower Brooches
Enamel, yellow gold, and diamonds

Flower Brooch
Enamel, yellow gold, and diamonds
Illustrated in *Paris [Exposition] 1889* with
diamond leaves

Thistle Stickpin
Enamel, yellow gold

Orchid Brooch
Enamel, yellow gold, and diamonds
Illustrated in *Paris [Exposition] 1889* with
additional blossoms

Clockwise from top left:

15. Vinaigrettes (two views)
Late 19th century
Signed by Tiffany & Co.

Decorated with a rattlesnake and a bird
Rock crystal, yellow gold, demantoid garnets, diamonds, pearls, and rubies

Decorated with a lizard and flies
Rock crystal, yellow gold, demantoid garnets, diamonds, and rubies

16. Acorn Vinaigrettes
Late 19th century
Signed by Tiffany & Co.

Smoky rock crystal, diamonds, yellow gold, and platinum, with pendant attachment

Rock crystal, silver, yellow gold, and diamonds with yellow-gold finger chain

17. Ivory Desk Ornaments
Late 19th century
Signed by Tiffany & Co.

Inkwell
Ivory, enamel, and yellow gold

Seal
Ivory, enamel, ruby, and yellow gold

Matchbox
Ivory, enamel, and yellow gold

18. Vinaigrette

(for scent or smelling salts)
Late 19th century

Rock crystal, amethyst, diamonds, and
yellow gold
Signed by Tiffany & Co.

Bangle
Late 19th century

Yellow gold, amethysts, zircons,
garnets, and "brown peridot"
(renamed sinhalite in 1952)
Signed by Tiffany & Co.

19. Vinaigrettes
Late 19th century
Signed by Tiffany & Co.

Vinaigrette in an abstract marine style
Rock crystal, yellow gold, enamel, and
diamonds

Heart-shaped vinaigrette with finger
chain
Rock crystal, platinum, yellow gold,
rubies, and diamonds

drew upon Russian, Hungarian, Turkish, Spanish, East Indian, Greek, Javanese, Japanese, French Renaissance, and Egyptian sources, to name just a few.

The city of Chicago was not untouched by the glamour of these jewelry exhibits. Two years later, J. Lebolt founded Lebolt Inc., which would become a venerable Chicago institution along with C. D. Peacock and Spaulding & Co. By 1903 Lebolt had an office in New York (at 54 West Twenty-third Street) and one in Paris. The firm specialized in pearls and diamond jewelry. Another important jewelry house— Lackritz—was founded in 1898 and sold fine jewelry in the popular styles of the period.

The 1900 Exposition in Paris

At the 1900 Exposition in Paris the exhibits by Tiffany & Co., Tiffany Glass & Decorating Co., and the Gorham Company were grouped opposite each other in the Department of Varied Industries. The Tiffany & Co. exhibit emphasized jewelry, with a continuation of the firm's previous themes: American Indian motifs were in evidence beside Pompeiian, Egyptian, Greek, Roman, Indian and medieval ones. Moreover, the firm again stressed that their jewels were produced by American craftsmen and that the materials (in most cases) were from American mines and fisheries. Among the gemstones highlighted in this exhibit were Montana sapphires, Mexican fire opals, and Maine tourmalines. This highly colorful and original display, distinguished by a series of huge, gem-set flowers (including a pink wild rose in Maine tourmalines and a bluish-purple iris in Montana sapphires) was in keeping with the exhibits presented by the French jewelers, René Lalique and Henri Vever, whose enamel jewels in the Art Nouveau style were causing a sensation. Most of the turn-of-the-century jewelers at the exposition were presenting provocative and unconventional displays. Tiffany & Co. followed suit with its life-size flower brooches set with American gems.

In his 1908 book *Jewellery*, the English historian H. Clifford Smith summed up Tiffany & Co.'s international reputation, "Messrs. Tiffany of New York have shown how artistic design may be combined with fine and rare gems—the natural instinct for which will have to be gratified so long as jewelry is worn."[17]

Wild rose branch
Photograph
From the scrapbook, Photographs:
Tiffany & Co. Exhibit: Paris Exhibition,
1900

"Wild Rose Branch. Pink Tourmalines,
Emeralds and Diamonds.
  "The spray of wild rose is made up of
pink tourmalines, set en masse on the
leaves of the flower to give the natural
color. The centre topaz is surrounded
by small diamonds to represent the little
calyxes as in nature. The main branch
or stem of the rose is of green gold. The
leaves are represented by emeralds
shaped to conform with the natural leaf.
  "There are 20 marquise emeralds, 62
pink tourmalines, 1 yellow topaz, 7
pear-shaped en cabochon emeralds
and 164 brilliants."

Chapter Four

Art Nouveau

Louis Comfort Tiffany

20. Art Nouveau Dragonfly Brooch
Early 20th century

Black opals, demantoid garnets, platinum, and yellow gold
Signed by Tiffany & Co.
Shown at the Louisiana Purchase Exposition, 1904; part of a group of jewels designed by Louis Comfort Tiffany

American design was considerably enlivened at the turn of the century by Charles Tiffany's son Louis Comfort Tiffany (1848–1933). Born in New York, Louis was an artistic child, whom his father rashly assumed would succeed him in the family business. Just as the senior Tiffany had sensed the needs of his contemporaries, so his son sensed the needs of his—and they had changed.

The luxurious palaces that had been built by architects such as William Morris Hunt were no longer simply in need of decorative objects and furnishings, important as these might be, but of someone to arrange the growing number of acquisitions. This demanded a certain deftness, for styles and periods were jumbled in most American collections. Louis Tiffany was qualified, by background and temperament, to pioneer in the unexplored field of interior decorating. He had studied painting seriously, at home and abroad, and had traveled extensively in Europe and North Africa.

At thirty-one Louis founded his own interior-design firm, Associated Artists. Its goal was to elevate the arrangement of interiors to the level of an art. He was not alone in his mission; Oscar Wilde had lectured on the topic in America in 1882 and 1883. James Abbott McNeill Whistler had finished his Peacock Room in London in 1877 and presented a Primrose Room at the 1878 Exposition in Paris.

Louis Tiffany's firm did not cater solely to a wealthy, international clientele. He also considered the aesthetic needs of the American people, professing to prefer them to the "the king, the noble, the millionaire."[1] This was an astute, as well as a philosophical, decision. The American middle classes were more affluent than ever before and very much in need of beautiful and useful decorative objects. Louis's original firm, which became the Tiffany Glass & Decorating Co., and later Tiffany Studios, offered the public a wide range of such objects in glass—a material he made famous.

The Jewels of Louis Comfort Tiffany

Enamel is powdered glass; its traditional association with jewelry piqued the interest and curiosity of Louis Comfort Tiffany. In the late 1890s he established two successive jewelry workshops: the first was in his mansion on Seventy-second Street, and the second was on Twenty-third Street. He staffed the latter with jewelers, repoussé workers, enamelers, and etchers under the direction of his enamelist, Julia Munson. For two years Louis devoted himself to enameled jewelry with the same singleminded attention he had previously given to his glass and stained-glass vases, windows, and lamps. He employed enamels from his own glassworks in Corona, New York.

The exhibits he presented at the 1904 Louisiana Purchase Exposition in St. Louis were successful. Thus, when Tiffany & Co. established an Artistic Jewelry Department on the sixth floor of their new premises at Fifth Avenue and Thirty-seventh Street, in 1905, they appointed Louis Comfort Tiffany its director; Julia Munson was his enamelist and overseer.

Art Nouveau Jewelry: Tiffany & Co.

The Artistic Jewelry Department at Tiffany & Co. was never very profitable. America was ambivalent about Art Nouveau jewelry, calling it New Art jewelry. *The Jewelers' Circular and Horological Review* cautiously stated, "It may be urged, perhaps, that it is more fitted for the case of the collector than for wear . . .".[2]

The most lavish of Louis Tiffany's jewels date from the early 1900s. The motifs of the 1904 Exposition, reported by *The Jewelers' Circular and Horological Review*, *The International Studio*, and *Vogue*, were the same as those utilized by the Art Nouveau jewelers of Europe. However, the flowers and themes from nature were American: a spray of spirea, a dandelion seed ball, wild carrot flowers, blackberries, the fruit of the mountain ash, and the solanum (a relative of the deadly nightshade). This style of jewelry was by now a tradition at Tiffany & Co.; it went back to the 1880s and the magnificent three-dimensional enamel flowers exhibited at the 1889 Exposition in Paris.

Louis Tiffany and another of the firm's designers, Paulding Farnam (a relative of C. T. Cook, the second president of the firm), were both identified with Art Nouveau jewelry through their use of enamels. Paulding Farnam also exhibited jewels at the 1904 Exposition in St. Louis, the most notable being a chain and pendant of diamonds set in gold with enamel.

Charles Lewis Tiffany died in 1902. He was succeeded as president by a longtime associate, C. T. Cook, who had joined the firm in 1848 as a delivery boy. Cook worked his way up through the firm, distinguishing himself in management. Under his direction the firm continued to pursue the course that had originally brought growth and fame to Tiffany & Co., namely the purveying of fine gems and jewelry.

Art Nouveau Jewelry: Marcus & Co.

A second fine jeweler, Marcus & Co., was identified in America with the turn-of-the-century styles shown in the 1900 Exposition in Paris. Charles Tiffany's former associate, Herman Marcus, was now a member of his son William's firm, Marcus & Co., located at 857 Broadway. A second son, George Elder Marcus, had joined them in the meantime.

Herman Marcus had always been respected for his connoisseurship, expressed in a thorough knowledge of painting, classical literature, and engraved gems—areas of study still associated with jewelers and gentlemen in the Old World. In Europe, the fashion for cameos, Etruscan style jewels, and all-diamond jewels had just come to an end, and in its place came an unexpected enthusiasm for Art Nouveau and, consequently, for floral patterns. Because of Herman's European background and connections, Marcus & Co. was aware of these new developments in style.

There is a story that a member of Marcus & Co. went to Paris to study *plique-à-jour* enameling with René Lalique, the renowned French jeweler and glass designer. Although the technique of *plique-à-jour* was used with dexterity on the Marcus & Co. pieces, they were too thin and delicate for wear, unlike Lalique's jewels. The American firm's admiration for Lalique, however, is exemplified in its remarkable series of flowers; the Marcus & Co. iris is fully three-dimensional.

This firm's interest in European Art Nouveau is also reflected in a second jewel that imitates the front of a pendant by the European designer Edward Colonna. (Colonna was a designer for Samuel Bing's gallery in Paris, "L'Art Nouveau," which gave its name to the movement.) Since Colonna had been in America in the 1880s (working with Louis Comfort Tiffany on the interior of the Ogden Goelet house), he may have come into contact with Herman Marcus there.

Themes from Nature

In the latter part of the nineteenth century, American jewelers were aware of the works of Oscar Wilde and the tenets of the Aesthetic Movement in England, and they adopted some of their motifs. *The Jewelers' Circular and Horological Review* reported

24. Art Nouveau Flower Jewels
1900
Signed by Marcus & Co.

Orchid Pendant
Plique-à-jour enamel, diamonds,
conch pearls, and platinum

Iris Brooch
Plique-à-jour enamel, yellow gold

that the heroine in "Patience," a Gilbert and Sullivan operetta that satirized Oscar Wilde, wore a dress decorated with storks, lizards, frogs, sunflowers, and lilies. The interest in such subjects was further enhanced in America by contemporary developments in the natural sciences and by the growing number of natural history collections in museums. A strange mixture of influences converged on jewelry in this period, and consequently, at the dawn of the twentieth century, designs for American jewelry were dominated by flowers, flies, bugs, bees, butterflies, lizards, sunbursts, and spiders. Some of these brooches and pendants became quintessential American jewels, such as the pansy in violet enamel with a diamond center. Applying painted enamels in deep hues was a popular American form of decoration, which was used on jeweled flowers. The enamel was painted over a white base and rendered matte in a dilute hydrofluoric acid bath.

Small, fine, and precious, these enameled and gem-set jewels were at first worn as brooches for securing the lace worn across dress bodices. Pins depicting winged creatures were made so that their attachments remained hidden when they were worn, which made them appear even more natural.

Dress

Victorian, Empire, Directoire, Neoclassical, and oriental influences characterized dress in the first decade of this century. Two Tiffany & Co. necklaces of the period provide an example of just how varied jewelry was at the time. The first is an openwork band of pale enamel with tiny turquoise, pearl, and diamond accents in a Louis XVI and Marie Antoinette mode; it was made to be worn with similarly styled gowns. The second necklace is composed of gems of exotic colors that were associated with the Orient.

In only two or three years' time, the Paris dressmaker Paul Poiret loosed "a few rough wolves—reds, greens, violets, royal blue"[3] on the "sheepcote"[4] of "tender blue hortensias, niles, maizes, straws, all that was soft,"[5] and in so doing, revolutionized female attire. As a result of the vogue for extravagant oriental styles, women put away their corsets; a new bodice line came into style, frequently a loose mass of folds that called for a long necklace.

As the colors employed by French dressmakers became more opulent and original, diamond jewelry regained prominence because of the neutral colors of the gems. The oriental influence, which stemmed from several factors—France's involvement in Morocco, the Turkish Wars, the Balkan crisis—was unabated. In June, 1910, the Ballets Russes presented *Scheherazade* with costumes and set designs by Leon Bakst.

Clockwise from top left:

25. Brooch with Pendant Attachment
With inscribed date, "1908"

Opals, yellow gold, platinum,
diamonds, and pearls
Signed by Marcus & Co.

**Post-Impressionist Brooch Depicting
Ship and Seascape**
Early 20th century

Opals, yellow gold, platinum,
diamonds, and pearls
Signed by Marcus & Co.

**26. Pansy Pendant Watch Brooch with
Chain**
Late 19th century

Inscribed, "Pittsburgh, PA"
Yellow gold, enamel, and diamonds
Unsigned

27. Cathedral Brooch
Early 20th century

Opals and yellow gold
Signed by Marcus & Co.

28. Dog Collar
With inscribed date, "1904"

Yellow gold, enamel, turquoise, pearls, and diamonds
Signed by Tiffany & Co.

29. Moorish Style Suite
Early 20th century

Claspless, latticework bracelet for the upper arm
Yellow gold, sapphires, diamonds, and enamel
Signed by Marcus & Co.

Two rings
Yellow gold, sapphires, diamonds, and enamel
Signed by Geo E. Marcus

30. Oriental-style Necklace
Early 20th century
(facing page)

Sapphires, rubies, emeralds, yellow gold, and enamel; on blue and green silk cords
Signed by Tiffany & Co.

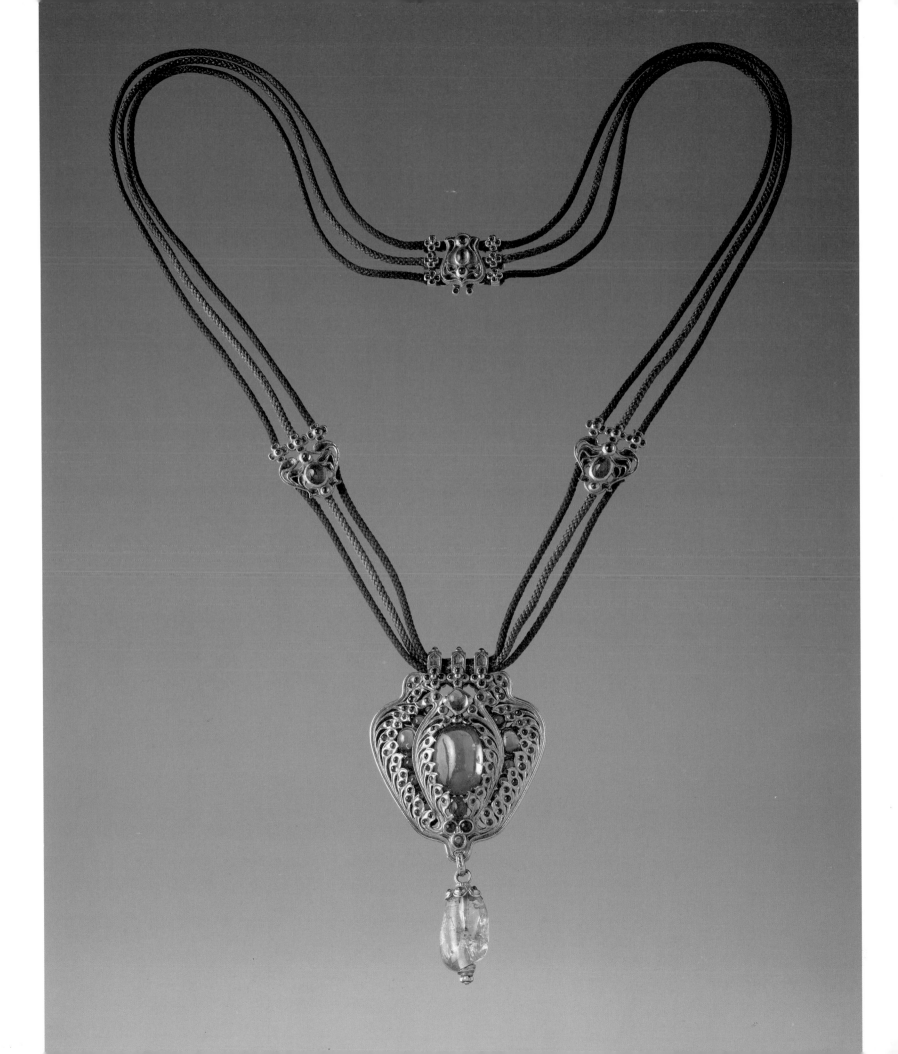

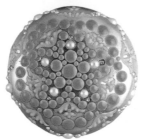

Clockwise from top left:

31. Gentleman's Watch
Early 20th century

Yellow gold, enamel, and onyx
cabochon
Signed by Dreicer & Co.

Sweet Box
Late 19th century

Yellow gold, enamel, diamonds,
and pearls
Signed by Tiffany & Co.

32. Card Case
Early 20th century

Yellow gold, enamel, diamonds, and
platinum
Signed by Tiffany & Co.

33. Brooches
Early 20 century
Signed by Tiffany & Co.
(top to bottom)

Lapis lazuli, yellow gold, and enamel

Amethyst, yellow gold, and enamel

Brown jade, yellow gold, and enamel
With inscribed date, "October, 1916"

Ceylon sapphires, yellow gold, and
enamel

Ceylon sapphires, green tourmaline,
and yellow gold filigree

This created a fashion for long necklaces, with medallions, plaques, and tassels, which became the preferred accessory on both sides of the Atlantic. The trailing furs, aigrettes, and turbans spelled the end of the utilitarian handy pin and of the practical jewelry associated with the previous styles. Their place was taken by diamond lorgnettes and watch pendants suspended from lengthy strands of diamond link-chains.

Jewelry Costuming

The continuing emphasis on using native gems and semiprecious stones did have an unexpected effect by the middle of the first decade of the twentieth century. Jewelers were admitting that the color of the stones—rather than their intrinsic value—was a determining factor in the success of their wares. They perceived that the color of a piece of jewelry could be matched to the color of a woman's gown. This proved effective in selling jewelry, and a term was coined to describe this matching of fabric and stone: jewelry costuming, a novel idea at that time.

The colors of stones were subjected to the scrutiny of the emerging fashion press. Conclusions were reached: Montana sapphires were appropriate for electric blue velvet; garnets for the winter shades of claret, burgundy, and wine; amethyst and kunzite for lavender reception gowns; moonstones for the soft silver grays; tourmalines for broadcloth and velvet; aquamarines for evening wear and calling costumes; and the opal matrix for dark gowns for street wear.

Semiprecious stones, originally popularized by Tiffany & Co., now came into vogue all over the nation. Mottled pink thomsonite, found on the shores of Lake Superior, a "stone seldom seen in the jeweler's shop,"[6] was considered to be in harmony with the new pink gowns, and American bluish-green chlorastrolite with the new green fabrics. These semiprecious stones were applied predominantly to brooches with practical applications, which were innumerable: lace pins, bonnet pins, jabot pins, automobile pins, and a general category of handy pin, used for securing a piece of lace, a shawl, a handkerchief, or bonnet ribbons. The success of jewelry costuming enabled jewelers' sales to double, treble, and quadruple.

What remains from this period is a host of highly original small jewels with unexpected color schemes. The motifs employed range from traditional flowers and grapes to Celtic motifs.

Watchcases and their attachments were substantially affected by jewelry costuming too. Under the influence of the workshops of Fabergé and Cartier, these were now engraved and tinted in soft-hued enamels. This technique is known as guilloche enamel. One watch from this period, in addition to utilizing the new colors that

34. Decorated Watches

Early 20th century
(top to bottom, left to right)

Yellow gold, enamel, diamonds, and platinum
Signed by Bailey, Banks & Biddle

Yellow gold, enamel, emerald, diamonds, and platinum
Signed Tiffany & Co.

Yellow gold, enamel, emerald, diamonds, and platinum
Signed by Marcus & Co.

Yellow gold, enamel, diamonds, and platinum
Signed by Tiffany & Co.

Depicting a round temple of love
Yellow gold, enamel, diamonds, emeralds, and platinum
Signed Tiffany & Co.

Yellow gold, enamel, and pearls
Signed Shreve, Crump & Low

Pendant watch brooch
Yellow gold, enamel, emeralds, diamonds, and platinum
Signed Tiffany & Co.

35. Commemorative Watch

Early 20th century

Depicting Wilbur Wright's historic flight over New York Harbor on September 30, 1909
Yellow gold, enamel, sapphires, ruby, diamond, and platinum
Engraved, "L.M."
Unsigned

harmonized with fabrics, depicted a major news event: it recorded Wilbur Wright's 50-mile-an-hour flight around the Statue of Liberty on September 30, 1909, an event of great notoriety. The flight, which lasted fifteen minutes, took place in a strong wind. It was a demonstration of Wright's advanced skill in aerial navigation. His feats included flying over water, circling the Statue of Liberty, and hovering over the outgoing *Lusitania*. The watchcase derives its design from a photograph that appeared on the cover of *Harper's Weekly* for October 9, 1909.

Arbiters of Style

By 1910, American jewelers had discovered a showcase for their work in American magazines. In the early twentieth century, *Vogue* magazine became an arbiter of fashion in the United States. *Vogue*'s publisher and owner, Condé Nast, directed his publication toward women of wealth and distinction, and began to entice manufacturers of luxury items to advertise in its pages. Fine jewelers, who had never considered this form of publicity, were soon advertising as well as featuring their jewelry in *Vogue*, knowing that they would reach their clientele.

The financial Panic of 1907 hit American jewelers hard and contributed to a return to the fashion for small jewels, utilizing semiprecious stones. The merits of press coverage became more apparent to retail jewelers in the wake of the Panic of 1907. *The Jewelers' Circular and Horological Review* ran an editorial entitled, "A Readjustment is not a Panic."[7]

The concept of jewelry costuming soon evolved into more than matching the color of a stone or enamel with a garment; it became the act of accessorizing an outfit with rings, brooches, necklaces, hair ornaments, earrings, and a decorated handbag. The art of wearing jewelry properly was demonstrated in a series of fully illustrated articles in *The Jewelers' Circular and Horological Review* that began on August 4, 1915. The series was entitled "First Principles in the Wearing of Jewelry: The Opening of An Educational Campaign That Will Help the Public and Benefit the Jeweler."[8] Both the jewelers and the fashion designers whose works were shown were given credit by name. This series was followed in 1916 by one entitled "The Latest Gowns and their Appropriate Adornment: How to Choose the Jewels to Accompany the Fall Wardrobe"[9] and by "The Latest Coiffure Modes and Hair Ornaments: How to Choose the Jewels Appropriate to Different Modes in Hair Dressing Called for by the New Styles."[10] These articles, which continued through 1917, were copyright free for the use of small newspapers and magazines across the United States. They contributed to the vogue for the discerning wearing of jewelry.

Chapter Five

Platinum Jewelry

The All-Diamond Style

As America grew more wealthy, diamond jewelry once again became increasingly popular. The diamond had been in short supply at the turn of the century, because of the South African, or Boer, War. With the resolution of the political situation, an all-diamond style—whiter than ever before—emerged. The new whiteness was the result of the use of platinum, which is a practically unoxidizable material. Until the eighteenth century, when Europe obtained diamonds from India, they had had to be bought in Europe from century-old diamond centers, or taken from crown jewels. Then, in 1725, diamonds were discovered in Brazil, a source that produced a good supply over the next 150 years. Diamonds were also found near the city of Kimberley in South Africa in 1871, and in the Vaal River in 1886.

At first the Kimberley mine was worked as a large open-pit mine. Growing knowledge about the formation of diamonds and advances in mining engineering, however, led to the use of underground mining techniques; this resulted in the discovery of the kimberlite pipes, in which diamonds are formed. As a result of this windfall, South Africa would produce 98 percent of the world's diamonds well into the twentieth century.

One exhibit among the Varied Industries (in the French section) at the 1904 Exposition in St. Louis was very popular with the American public. It contained a collection of diamonds in over seventy shades and colors, the largest group of diamonds ever shown by the Parisian dealer A. Eknayan at an exposition. Their American agents in New York were J. Dreicer & Son, which would be identified with fine American jewelry for the next quarter of a century.

The mating of diamonds and platinum in the new all-diamond style was revolutionary; each material enhanced the unique properties of the other. This style has also been the twentieth century's most significant contribution, so far, to the history of jewelry.

36. Necklace
Late 19th century

Fancy-colored diamonds, yellow gold, and platinum
Signed by Tiffany & Co.

37. Ring
Early 20th century

Emeralds, diamonds, yellow gold, and
platinum
With presentation inscription, "Edith C.
Macy from Editha April 21, 1903"
Signed by Tiffany & Co.

38. Decorated Watches
Late 19th and early 20th centuries
(clockwise from left)

With inscribed date, "Christmas, 1905"
Pendant watch brooch
Diamonds, demantoid garnets, yellow
gold, and platinum
Signed Tiffany & Co.

Pendant watch brooch
Diamonds, half-pearls, and
yellow gold
Signed Tiffany & Co.

Pendant watch brooch
Diamonds, yellow gold, and platinum
Signed Tiffany & Co.

Diamonds, yellow gold, and platinum
Signed Black, Starr & Frost

The History of Platinum

Platinum was first discovered and recorded in South America during the Spanish Conquest. The conquistadors brought the metal back to Europe in the sixteenth century. The early samples of platinum did not excite scholarly and technical minds at the courts of Europe. The metal was named *platina*, a diminutive for silver (*plata*), which immediately classified the new metal, putting it in a lowly position. This was the result of the native Indians' opinion of the metal: to them it was "unripe gold"; they threw it back into the river when they found it.

European chemists of the early eighteenth century saw platinum as a strange, infusible, heavy metal. It was resistant to oxidation (the black discoloration of metal associated with tarnished silver), and to caustic chemicals—and equally resistant to scientific analysis. With the advent of quantitative analysis, in addition to studying the elements and their proportions in a specific alloy or ore, chemists were able to isolate platinum as a single metal in a group of seven allied metals: platinum, palladium, iridium, rhodium, ruthenium, and osmium.

Platinum Jewelry

Historically Russia has been identified with platinum, because of the large deposits found in the Ural Mountains. However, as a group, it was French jewelers—the finest and most progressive in the world in the early nineteenth century—who recognized its potential for fine jewelry. They liked the way platinum looked with diamonds; its bluish-white color retained a bright, polished finish that resisted oxidation. However, jewelers were unable to melt or fuse platinum in their workshops with the heating sources available; therefore, platinum was not commonly used in jewelry at this date. As a raw material, it was too difficult for nineteenth-century jewelers to work.

The History of the Jeweler's Torch

For thousands of years jewelers had been using a mouth blowpipe with an alcohol or oil lamp to melt metals. The jeweler blew into a flame with this apparatus in order to control the direction, size, and heat of the flame. Depending on the amount of oxygen his breath contained, the heat rose or fell.

But platinum, with a melting point of 1772°C (3217°F), was unaffected by this process. In contrast, the melting point of gold is only 1064°C (1945°F).

Advertisement for the Hoke torch

The Jewelers' Circular and Horological Review, November 26, 1919, p. 184

The nineteenth century made few innovations in the use of the blowpipe. Illuminating, or city, gas was installed in New York in the 1830s, enabling jewelers to use a gas burner rather than an alcohol lamp in their workshops, but even this did not provide sufficient heat to melt platinum.

Until the advent of bottled oxygen, the heat necessary to melt platinum could not be generated in a jeweler's workshop. In 1877 a Swiss and a French chemist, Raoul-Pierre Pictet and Louis-Paul Cailletet, simultaneously discovered a way to liquefy oxygen and store it in pressurized steel cylinders. This led to the creation of the jeweler's torch as it is known today.

The torch made all-platinum jewelry possible. By 1912 Sam W. Hoke of New York had developed and patented several torches to be used with oxygen and regular city gas. (They were called oxy-gas blowpipes in the beginning—an indication of how conservative jewelers were.) An important feature of these torches was the regulator, which kept oxygen pressure exactly uniform no matter how many torches were in use on the same gas lines. With the torch gold alloys of different carats could be hard-soldered faster and easier, and platinum welding became possible for the first time.

In the first examples of diamond-and-platinum jewelry, platinum sheet metal was soldered on top of a gold base. The diamonds were set into the platinum plate. The result seems heavy and cumbersome compared to the later all-platinum jewels; however, because of platinum's strength, ductility, and great durability, far less precious metal was required to make a fine jewel. Moreover, the settings became very delicate.

The Platinum Style

The most popular jewels in this new style were dog collars, bow brooches, latticework bodice ornaments, and lavalieres (named after Duchess Louise de la Vallière, one of the favorites of Louis XV). The sources for jewelry designs came from French, English, and Spanish court dress of earlier centuries. The first platinum-and-diamond jewels were composed predominantly of small diamonds, and the designs were highlighted with calibre-cut sapphires and rubies.

The Challenge of European Jewelry

In America, a demand for great art and magnificent jewelry developed simultaneously. The trend in American taste had turned to the extravagant court styles of another age: at the marriage of the American heiress Helen Gould, one of the gifts she received (which was described in the February, 1913, *Jewelers' Circular and Horological Review*) was a diamond bowknot 12 inches wide with ribbons 1 inch thick.

French jewelers were generally still considered the best, and Americans traveling abroad accounted for half of these jewelers' yearly income. The collection of duty on these articles was erratic and hard to enforce. It was difficult for officials to distinguish new purchases from travelers' prior possessions. Barely any records of duties collected exist in the U.S. Treasury. Yet smuggling grew: some of it innocent; some of it devious. This period, 1900–20, has been called The Golden Age of Smuggling in America. In 1912 the Ways and Means Committee proposed an amendment to allow jewelry purchased as gifts to enter the country free of duty. This encouraged "the tourist smugglers"[1] and acted against the best interests of the jewelry trade. These events perpetuated Americans' desire to buy fine jewelry abroad. In the minds of most Americans, when one of the Parisian jewelry houses decided to open a branch in New York, they were still identified with the finest work.

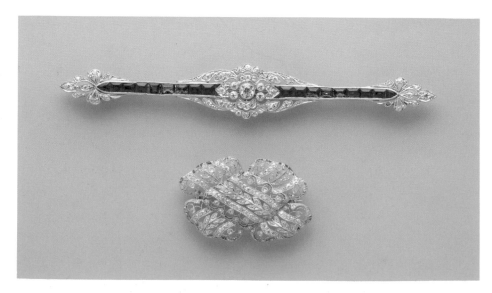

Cartier, New York

In 1909 Cartier, New York opened at 712 Fifth Avenue, fully prepared to provide to Americans at home, as they had been doing in Paris with great success, the platinum jewelry that was becoming increasingly fashionable. Cartier, New York carried an excellent line of pieces in the new platinum-and-diamond style.

Only the most advanced workshops were capable of producing platinum-and-diamond jewels at this point. The ability to work platinum was considered a specialty and differentiated from the ability to work gold. Thus success was assured to any workshop or craftsman with advanced knowledge in this area.

Prominent New York Manufacturing Jewelers

In New York City at this time there were several large jewelry manufacturing firms. Changes in the working environment and in production methods were dramatic during the early twentieth century. In New York and other major American cities, electricity had brought new means of lighting and new equipment, including electric lathes, polishing lathes, and drill presses. The jeweler's workshop became more efficient, and jewelry workmanship more precise.

One of the most prominent American manufacturing jewelers was William Scheer, Inc. William Scheer had emigrated from Germany at the age of sixteen, apprenticed in Cincinnati, Ohio, and gone to New York to start his own enterprise. His business became the biggest in the country and supplied jewelry to retail firms across the United States. The jewelry was distributed by a large group of traveling salesmen, who returned to New York with information about the tastes and needs of the clients in their territory, as well as with custom orders for individuals.

The firms of Walter P. McTeigue (founded in 1895) and of Jacob Mehrlust were also important. The latter's firm had both an Uptown office, a factory (at 6 West Forty-eighth Street), and a Downtown office (at 12–14 John Street).

Oscar Heyman and his younger brother Nathan emigrated to New York from northwestern Russia: they had grown up in Goldingen, a village on the Baltic Sea. In 1901 the two brothers, thirteen and fifteen years old, had been sent to the Ukraine to work as apprentices in an uncle's jewelry workshop. Five years later they returned home for a brief reunion before emigrating to America.

The Heyman brothers arrived in America in 1906 with jewelry-making skills and a knowledge of how to work platinum, which enabled Oscar Heyman to obtain a job in Cartier, New York's first workshop at 712 Fifth Avenue. Oscar worked there for four

42. Tassel Pendant Necklace
Circa 1920
(opposite)

Pearls, sapphires, diamonds, and
platinum
Signed by Cartier, New York

43. Tassel Pendant Necklace
Circa 1920

Pearls, sapphires, diamonds, and
platinum
Unsigned

Ring
Pre-World War I

Diamonds, sapphires, and platinum
Signed Tiffany & Co.

44. Diamond Necklaces
(opposite, left to right)

Late 1920s
Detaches to form a collar or four line
bracelets
Diamonds and platinum
Signed by J.E. Caldwell & Co.

World War I
Diamonds, pearls, and platinum
Signed by J.E. Caldwell & Co.

45. Tassel Pendant Necklace
Circa 1920

Pearls, diamonds, and platinum
Unsigned

Ring
World War I

Diamonds and platinum
Unsigned

46. Patriotic Jewels

Flag Brooch
World War II
Diamonds, rubies, sapphires, and
platinum
Signed and retailed by J.E. Caldwell
& Co.
Manufactured by Oscar Heyman &
Bros., Inc.

Watch
World War I
Diamonds, rubies, sapphires, and
platinum
Unsigned

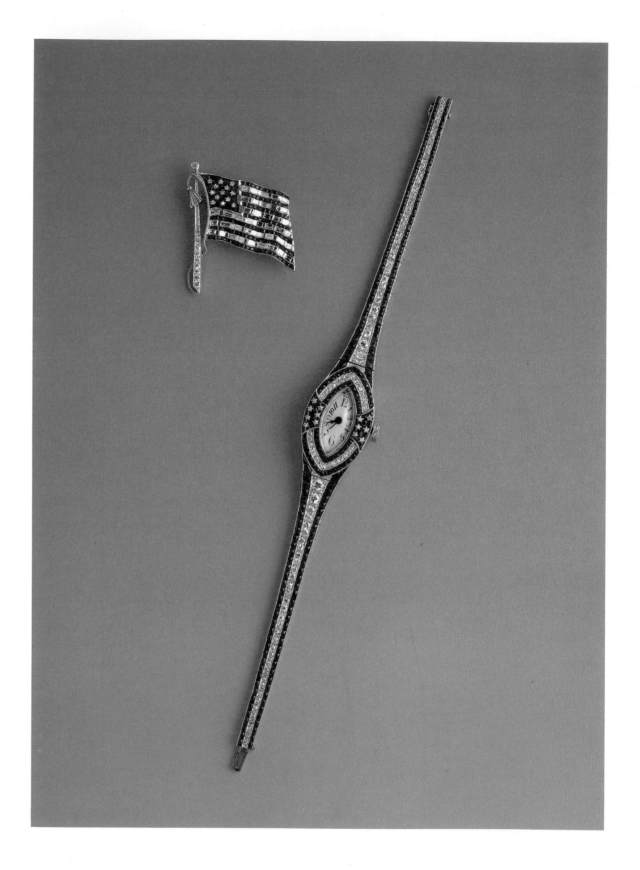

years, before establishing Oscar Heyman & Co. in 1912 with his brother Nathan. When the rest of the family emigrated to the United States, the firm became Oscar Heyman & Brothers, Inc.

As New York's manufacturing jewelers increased in size, the demand for ever finer jewelry was growing apace in America; thus jewelers' skills and their ability to produce such pieces advanced correspondingly.

Platinum and Patriotism

World War I forced the jewelry industry into the defensive. The problem centered around obtaining platinum: 90 percent of the world's supply came from Russia through Europe; the rest came from Colombia and Canada. During World War I and the Russian Revolution, the supply was limited and upon occasion, cut off entirely, for platinum was a necessary catalyzing agent in many chemical processes that might otherwise occur too slowly to be of any practical use in the war effort—for example, the production of highly concentrated sulphuric acid, employed in the manufacture of explosives. Because of platinum's importance to national defense, jewelers were asked to limit the production of jewelry that used platinum. The metal was now classified under the Explosives Act and came under the jurisdiction of the Bureau of Mines, which was influenced considerably by a strong chemical engineering lobby.

A conflict ensued, incited by the press. The cast of characters included jewelers, chemists, and overzealous patriotic "women against platinum jewelry." The jewelers formed the Jewelers' Vigilance Committee and the Jewelers' War Service Committee. These two groups worked closely with the chemical division of the War Service Board to explain the government's needs to jewelers and vice versa.

The public, which was only slightly informed about the platinum controversy, received all its information from the press, which emphasized that the metal was needed for munitions. What the press failed to explain was that platinum was a catalyst—it did not enter into the processes in which it was employed—consequently, the supply available should have been sufficient for the needs of both government and industry. The jewelry trade's problems were real and anticipated, so jewelers were embattled and fighting back.

Their classification as a luxury trade, and therefore as a nonessential industry, meant that their access to both fuel and transportation was threatened. In actual fact, jewelers did not suffer from a lack of either of them; however, their electric signs had to be turned off after business hours to save fuel at the electric power plants, and jewelers' opening hours at holidays were greatly reduced. Their labor force, like everyone else's, was depleted; and supplies were scarce and uncertain. When the government commandeered all unused metallic platinum, on March 12, 1918, works in progress and finished jewelry were exempt. This prompted jewelers to go into full production to escape what appears, in retrospect, to have been an unnecessarily harsh edit.

A further aspect of American jewelers' wartime experience was the curtailment of foreign trade, lessened to some degree in June of 1918 when the government—realizing that the dollar had fallen in value and needed boosting—called on jewelers to open up new markets and to remedy the situation by shipping goods from San Francisco and New York to ports in Central and South America. Moreover, unexpected places such as Egypt now became possible export markets.

The attitude of America's jewelers during World War I is characterized by the following quotation from an advertising circular of the period, "If you intend to be in business when the war is over, you must stay in business while the war is going on. As a merchant and businessman, you must 'carry on' actively, aggressively."[2]

All restrictions were lifted when the war ended on November 11, 1918, but the measure did not take effect until December 1, 1918—Christmas sales soared that year.

White Gold

The confusion of the war years accelerated experiments with metals, directed principally at finding a substitute for platinum. In order to fulfill the requirements of fashion at the time, the substitute had to be white.

Even before the outbreak of World War I, experiments had been underway to explore the bleaching properties of both nickel and palladium which, when alloyed with fine gold, turn that metal white. Researchers had been working on this project in America, England, and Germany. The results proved that the nickel-gold alloy, while very white, was extremely hard and lacked the ductility of platinum (its ability to bend without cracking). This made it less desirable as a setting for stones. The palladium gold alloy, while not as white as the nickel-gold one, was softer and thus easier to use as stone settings. Refiners and jewelers would continue to experiment with these alloys, becoming more conversant with their properties as this century progressed.

A second development of the war years was the displacement of craftsmen and workers into wartime industries, principally machine-oriented ones. As they returned to jewelry workshops, they introduced the mechanical knowledge and precision that enabled the jewelry industry to enter the Machine Age.

Chapter Six

The New York Jewelry Establishment
World War I to 1929

Search for a Style

47. **Brooches**
Early 1920s

Swan Brooch
Enamel, white and yellow gold, diamonds, sapphires, rubies, and peridots
Unsigned

Circle Brooch with pendant attachment
Carved jade, sapphires, and platinum
Signed by Dreicer & Co.

48. **Brooch**
World War I

Yellow sapphire, platinum, demantoid garnets, diamonds, and yellow gold
Unsigned

Since the turn of the century, jewelry manufacturing and retailing had ceased to be run primarily as small businesses; jewelry was big business now. Three well-known members of the trade in New York were worth over a million dollars and were cited in the *New York Herald Tribune*. Mentioned in its survey of millionaires in 1892 were Charles T. Cook, Charles L. Tiffany, and Louis C. Tiffany—all members of Tiffany & Co.

The Armory Show, which opened in New York on February 17, 1913, jolted the press and made Americans aware of modern art. When paintings by Picasso, Matisse, Duchamp, Cézanne, Léger, and Picabia were first seen, all the major American newspapers and magazines expressed shock. The potential of these revolutionary European works, their vibrant colors, straight lines, and angles, was recognized by designers in all fields. Impressionist painters were also reevaluated; their poetical approach and fondness for nature inspired a group of jewelry with landscape as its principal theme.

American jewelers had first been exposed to these new ideas just as World War I was beginning. The war abruptly cut off their communication with Europe. The dominant Parisian influence, which had kept jewelry seasonal and up to date, was removed too. In its absence, American jewelers were forced to create their own styles to excite their customers' interest.

The editor of *Vogue*, Edna Woolman Chase, solved the predicament of America's isolation from Paris by staging the first fashion show in America: the Fashion Fête of November 4, 1914. It was an exhibition of designs created by New York fashion houses and presented on living models for the benefit of French charities. It was such a success that *Vogue* sponsored another the following year. This fashion show was a playlet at the Palace Theater, New York; in the scenario a seamstress falls asleep at her work in a fashionable modiste's shop. In the ensuing dream, she finds herself fully dressed in the street, at the country club, and at a ball, where she is wearing $750,000 worth of diamond-and-platinum jewelry, including a tiara, collar, finger ring, and a 10-foot diamond chain by the New York jeweler E. M. Gattle, composed of 335 diamonds.

In America and abroad, art collections had always been taken seriously. Up-to-date presentations of the collections were thought to be beneficial to the country and to those in the design professions. The Armory Show of 1913 had exposed Americans to modern European painting, but the absorption of the new trends had been cut short by the outbreak of World War I. In 1917, to stimulate innovative design, the Metropolitan Museum of Art inaugurated its series of exhibits of modern manufactured objects. These were meant to encourage young designers and manufacturers to look at museum collections for inspiration. In its 1920 *Bulletin*, the Metropolitan Museum of Art reported the results, "It is therefore no longer a novelty to those who had to do with the industrial arts exhibition at the Metropolitan Museum to find an advertising design which originated in an ecclesiastical vestment, a furniture color which was found in Persian tiles, silverwork which saw its beginnings in carved ivories, a talcum powder box the design for which was suggested by Japanese prints, cravats which were designed after studies made in the armor collection."[1]

New York Retail Jewelers

Throughout the country, firms that were already well-established or taking shape would continue to prosper in this period. New York was then—and would continue to be—an important center for the jewelry industry. Tiffany & Co. and Black, Starr & Frost were the preeminent New York jewelers. Udall & Ballou was founded there in 1888. Herman Marcus had left Tiffany & Co. in the meantime and joined his son William E. Marcus at Jaques & Marcus (which became Marcus & Co. in 1892); and Theodore B. Starr had been in business under his own name since 1877.

The most successful New York jewelry retailers continued to move Uptown in Manhattan. By 1907, Tiffany & Co., Black, Starr & Frost, and Marcus & Co. had all left their premises in the Downtown area and moved to a more prestigious area, where the occupants of "phactons [sic.], victorias, barouches and broughams"[2] could see the wares in their windows. They settled on Fifth Avenue, from Thirty-third Street to Forty-seventh Street. Nor could the high rents in that area keep them from moving.

These firms—already venerable—were surrounded by other successful retail jewelers: Udall & Ballou, Dreicer & Co., E. M. Gattle, Thomas Kirkpatrick. All of them had been founded in the latter part of the nineteenth century. Only the firm of Theodore B. Starr continued at its premises on Twenty-fifth Street. The list above is a compendium of the finest New York jewelers of this time.

Cartier, New York

Cartier, New York was widely known for its superior platinum jewels and natural oriental pearl necklaces. Since early in the century, pearl necklaces had been the most coveted possessions of chic American and European women. An example of the esteem for this jewel is the famous Cartier pearl necklace, which the firm exchanged for a mansion on Fifth Avenue. The banker Morton Plant and Pierre Cartier concluded their swap in 1916, and Cartier, New York acquired their new premises at Fifth Avenue and Fifty-second Street.

Natural, white saltwater pearls from the Orient came to Europe from the island of Bahrain in the Persian Gulf, from Ceylon, and from Australia. Black pearls were obtained from Tahiti and Panama. Jacques Cartier, the son of the company's founder, traveled directly to the Persian Gulf to obtain the best specimens, and the firm had a fulltime agent in Bombay, India, the historic trading center for pearls in the Far East. When a perfect round pearl was found anywhere in the world Cartier, New York was alerted through Cartier, Paris. There was an international waiting list of the firm's clients for the strands that were assembled painstakingly year after year. Cartier, New York was identified with the finest in pearl necklaces.

Dreicer & Co., Inc.

Dreicer & Co. (whose beautiful black marble and brass-fitted building at 560 Fifth Avenue epitomized the latest fashion in jewelry establishments) rivaled Cartier, New York and the greatest Parisian jewelry houses from 1910 to the mid-1920s with its platinum jewelry and lavish pearl necklaces. This New York firm also had a branch in the Blackstone Hotel, Chicago.

In the late 1910s and early 1920s, Dreicer & Co. had been the first to introduce in New York the new experimental diamond cuts emanating from Paris. The firm bought a large quantity of French-cut square diamonds, which they used in novel flexible box bracelets.

In 1923, just a few years after the untimely death of Michael Dreicer, the founder's son, on July 26, 1921, the business was liquidated. For his courage and daring, Michael was later compared to the great Harry Winston, who would be the most widely publicized diamond dealer from the 1930s onward. Both men in their time introduced Americans to the finest diamond jewelry that could be obtained on either side of the Atlantic, taking financial risks, buying expensive stones, and setting new trends in jewelry design. It is unfortunate that Michael's father Jacob died shortly after his son, which caused the firm to close. Former employees of Dreicer & Co. went on to form a firm called Wedderien (eventually located at Madison Avenue and Fifty-second Street). The new firm included the watchmaker A. Wedderien, the buyer Edie Case, the jeweler R. Hellstern, and the pearl stringer Minnie Cosgrow.

The Founding of Raymond C. Yard, Inc.

The death of Michael Dreicer created a need for another individual jeweler of stature in the American jewelry industry. In 1922 Raymond C. Yard left his job as a salesman at Marcus & Co. to establish a retail firm upstairs at 607 Fifth Avenue. He wanted it to be small and discreet, capable of furnishing complete service to those who appreciated the finest in jewelry. Yard had a very select following which depended upon his excellent taste and outstanding ability to acquire the highest-quality precious stones and to mount them appropriately. (His first project was to furnish the jewelry for an upcoming Rockefeller wedding.)

E. M. Gattle

The New York firm E. M. Gattle, founded in the nineteenth century by Emanuel Gattle and well-established by the turn of the century, had a different orientation. This retail jeweler was associated with stars of the theater and the opera: the firm was initially located in the theater district on Broadway. In 1907 E. M. Gattle (located on Fifth Avenue at Thirty-eighth Street) opened a magnificent retail store devoted entirely to jewelry. Enrico Caruso was responsible for a measure of this firm's popularity. He ordered a ring in honor of his performance in *Rigoletto*; the result was a wide platinum band with three diamonds—bluish-white, canary, and brown—across the top. The E. M. Gattle design was a great success, and Caruso would not allow it to be reproduced. Later the firm published, in a small pamphlet, Caruso's letter to them, photographs of the tenor in his role as "the Duke," and the *Rigoletto* ring.

E. M. Gattle advertised as goldsmiths and platinumsmiths exclusively; no silverware, bric-a-brac, or curios were sold on its premises.

Business Between the World Wars

The end of World War I marked a new beginning for jewelers in America. Wartime controversy had given free publicity to the jewelry industry and prompted people to buy platinum jewels, hoping that the dwindling supply of the metal would increase its value.

In 1919 the business year opened profitably; everyone was busy ordering jewelry for what promised to be a magnificent year. Notable New York firms such as Cartier, New York; Dreicer & Co., E. M. Gattle, and Tiffany & Co. were using the Metropolitan Opera as a showcase; they worked right up to each opening night to prepare jewels for the stars in the audience as well as on the stage.

Jewelry was lavish at this period, harking back to an earlier mode—a former editor of *Vogue*, Jessica Daves, noted that fashionable photographs of Mrs. Astor in 1910 and 1918 were very much alike, ". . . there was not enough change to make a nonprofessional eye look twice."[3] The same could be said of fine jewelry.

Immediately after World War I, jewelers went back to Paris to see the new styles. At various times, when the American jewelry industry needed fresh inspiration to win a new generation of patrons, the jewelers looked to a foreign source: imported oriental goods from the China trade, European crown jewels, *plique-à-jour* enamel, or the Cubist painters of the 1913 Armory Show in New York.

From the Reconstruction era on, American jewelry workshops had been growing in number and were capable of supplying retail jewelers all over the country with well-made jewelry. The stumbling block was design. In the 1920s, American jewelers had to sustain the interest of a large number of new patrons who had become world travelers and were buying furiously from their French competitors.

Branch offices were opening fast to take advantage of the new international movements. Marcus & Co. advertised its branches in London, Paris, and Palm Beach. Udall & Ballou mentioned locations in Palm Beach, Florida; on Bellevue Avenue in Newport, Rhode Island; and at 48 Rue Lafayette, Paris in its advertisements. Black, Starr & Frost Inc. also had branches in Palm Beach and Southhampton, Long Island. The New York firm Charlton & Co. (founded in 1909 and located opposite St. Patrick's Cathedral at Fifth Avenue and Fifty-first Street) had branches in Palm Beach too and at 1 Rue de la Paix in Paris.

An example of the internationality of jewelers in the 1920s was provided by the French jeweler Arnold Ostertag. He came to New York in mid-October and then spent two months working in Los Angeles. Afterward he traveled to Florida, returning to

Cannes via Paris in time to work on the Riviera for Easter. After two months in Paris, Ostertag left to spend the summer months working in Deauville in July, in the south of France in August, and in Biarritz in September.

Tutankhamen and the American Woman

The enthusiasm with which manufacturers and designers had responded to the challenge of museum and other exhibitions revealed a receptivity to art and artifacts that would characterize this decade.

The Metropolitan Museum of Art had been attempting to elevate public taste with exhibitions of art from different periods, but by 1923 it became evident that what really fascinated the public was archeology.

The tomb of Tutankhamen had been discovered in the fall of 1922. Excavations and explorations at Luxor in Egypt, Uxmal in the Yucatán, and at Ur of the Chaldees on the Euphrates were bringing to light whole civilizations. Lord Carnarvon, Howard Carter, Sylvanus Griswold Morley, Sir Arthur Evans, and Sir Charles Leonard Woolley were explaining their finds in lavishly illustrated periodicals as well as in scholarly tracts. They were also hosts to Americans who traveled to the sites.

These great excavations were news worldwide, and news makes fashion. Ancient designs entered into the jewelry vocabulary almost immediately, influencing everything from line bracelets to vanity cases. The line bracelets became the jeweler's archeological showpieces. Border motifs were taken from ancient civilizations and translated into precious and semiprecious stones and into enamel work. In some instances, pictorial images and hieroglyphs were depicted in specially cut stones. The bracelets became increasingly complex and charming. As the appreciation of this style grew, such jewels were worn juxtaposed, as though they were marching up the bare arms of modern women.

In April, 1923, *Vogue* proclaimed, "The Mode Has a Rendezvous by the Nile." The 1920s' woman saw herself mirrored in the tomb paintings of Thebes: like her Egyptian sisters, she was tall and slender; she wore pleated skirts, sandals with straps, and Egyptian style jewelry. The Egyptian style jewelry in the next month's issue of *Vogue* was attributed to Theodore B. Starr. It was one of the last collections to be publicized by the firm before it went out of business.

The French Industrial Exhibit, New York (1924)

On May 15, 1924, Americans at the French Industrial Exhibit previewed the new jewelry of the preeminent Parisian firms Cartier, Paris; Boucheron, and Mauboussin (founded in 1827), a French court jeweler and one of the most important and modern of the French firms. With branches in Paris, Rio de Janeiro, and Buenos Aires, Mauboussin was planning to establish another branch in New York. Its latest collection included broad pictorial bracelets, huge brooches, jabot and bar pins, and shoulder tassels. The work of all three of these French firms showed the new combinations of onyx, turquoise, coral, and diamonds; jewelry in the widely acclaimed Egyptian style was also represented in their displays. Each evening for the duration of the exhibit, French models presented clothes in sport, street, and evening styles by Worth, Callot sisters, Paquin, Vionnet, Jenny, Lanvin, and Drecoll, accessorized with the latest French jewelry.

Exposition des Arts Décoratifs, Paris (1925)

American jewelers' continuing search for a distinctly American style seemed to pass unnoticed. The American government, unlike the French one, did not support the arts nor luxury trades. When an invitation to participate in the 1925 Exposition arrived, Herbert Hoover, the American secretary of Commerce, declined, after he had conferred with various heads of industry. Hoover stated, ". . . they did not consider that we could contribute sufficiently varied design of unique character or of special expression in American artistry to warrant such a participation."[4]

Those most affected by Hoover's decision were so dismayed that they requested the formation of a commission to report on the exposition—unlike other members of the commission, the representatives of the jewelry and fashion industries were not overly impressed by what they saw, for they had been going to Paris regularly since the end of the war. Walter P. McTeigue of the New York Jewelry Crafts Association, the representative of the jewelry industry, was tepid in his praise, "The jewelry exhibits at the Exposition were, as might have been expected, of great richness and beauty."[5] He commented on the scale of the work and the materials, "Perhaps the most notable feature about the jewelry as a whole from the American standpoint was the considerable number of large pieces in the form of brooches, pendants, drops and girdle tassels that contained very few precious stones, but gained their effect through semiprecious materials like black onyx, coral, turquoise matrix and enamels, that were of such size as to form a decorative element of the costume."[6]

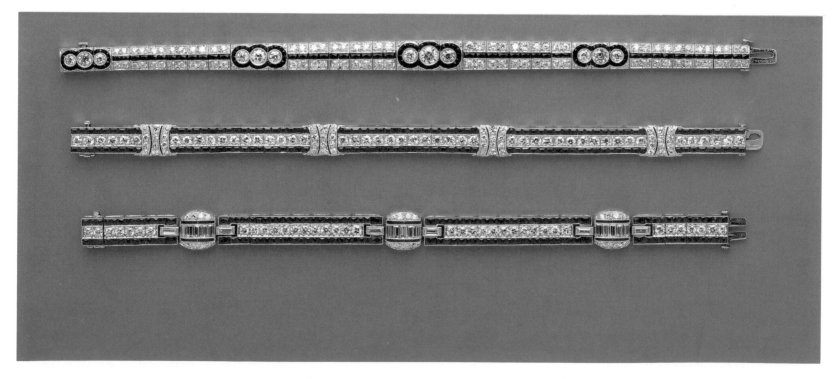

49. Multiple Bracelets
1920s
(opposite, top to bottom)

Slave link bracelet
Emeralds, diamonds, and platinum
Signed Black, Starr & Frost

Flexible box bracelet
Diamonds and platinum
Signed Tiffany & Co.

Bracelet
Diamonds, emeralds, and platinum
Signed by Cartier, New York

Flexible box bracelet
Diamonds, onyx, and platinum
Signed Tiffany & Co.

Flexible box bracelet
Rubies, diamonds, and platinum
Unsigned

Flexible box bracelet
Diamonds, sapphires, and platinum
Manufactured by William Scheer, Inc.

This page, clockwise from top:

50. Jardiniere Brooch
1930

Rock crystal, diamonds, emeralds,
sapphires, rubies, black enamel, and
platinum
Signed by Cartier, New York

Temple of Love Brooch
1920s

Diamonds, emeralds, and platinum
Unsigned

51. Brooch
World War I

Rock crystal, diamonds, emeralds,
platinum, and yellow gold
Signed by Tiffany & Co.

**52. Pendant Brooch with Stylized
Islamic Motif**
1920s

Diamond, sapphires, onyx, and
platinum
Signed by Cartier, New York

53. Pendant Necklace
(detail)
1920s

Rock crystal, diamonds, and platinum
Signed by Charlton & Co.

54. Jabot Pin with Indian Motif
1920s

Crystal, diamonds, onyx, and platinum
Unsigned

Watch Pendant
1920s

Diamonds, onyx, enamel, and
platinum
Signed by Charlton & Co.

Brooch with Stylized Indian Motif
1925

Diamonds, black enamel, and
platinum
Signed by Cartier, New York

The reactions of journalists and jewelry designers to the exposition were jubilant. Earlier in the century jewelry had been linked to costume and treated as a fashion accessory; now it was considered a branch of the decorative arts.

For those who discussed and designed jewelry, a new era was dawning. Jewelers broadened their themes to include modern architecture, painting, sculpture, furniture design, interior decoration, and textiles. Egyptian and Cubist art, patchwork quilts, Spanish openwork grills, Persian miniatures, East Indian jewelry, American Indian pottery, landscapes, and aerial views also began to play a part in the creation of jewelry designs.

This odd blending of geometrical shapes and archeological motifs—identified with the 1925 Exposition—had first appeared in fabrics, hats, parasols, bags, sashes, belts, slippers, fans, and hosiery. The effect was so novel that the closest parallel seemed to be in the new music—jazz. This designation was promptly adopted; and in jewelry, jazz motifs included not only geometrical patterns, zigzags, and polka dots, but also exuberant, stylized flowers. Color was part of the designs too. The original flowers for these designs emanated from various embroidery firms in Paris; they were rendered in outlandish hues—reds, purples, greens, and yellows. These orchids, wild roses, pansies, and lilies created a polychromatic style that could be worked out in enamel and semiprecious stones—lapis lazuli, jade, coral, onyx, moonstone, and amethyst—which were cut to fit the designs.

From the outset, French jewelers realized that jewelers of other nationalities would admire their patterns, analyze their techniques, and adapt their ideas. Their exhibits represented the modern style to everyone.

Now *Vogue* took its readers to the Rue de la Paix—the street of the Parisian jewelers—whereas two years before, it had taken them to Tutankhamen's tomb. American women were depicted wearing the most lavish of jewels—the only drawback being that many of them were European.

American jewelers had suffered a setback by not exhibiting in Paris. Yet many American jewelers maintained buying offices in that city. These offices bought gems, perused new designs by French designers in American employ, and ordered French clocks and boxes, for the enamelwork on them could not be done profitably in New York, where neither tradition, skills, nor labor force existed which could produce the very special effects found on these beautiful objects. A single French workshop, Verger Frères, at 51 Rue Sainte-Anne, supplied clocks, watches, objets d'art, jewelry, and trophies to the finest jewelers in America.

All the new sketches coming into the buying offices in Paris emphasized polychromatic effects. Considering the fashion and preference in America for gems

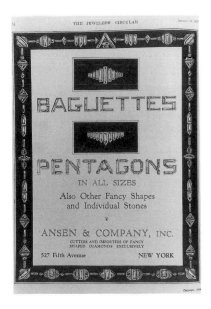

Advertisement for baguette diamonds

The Jewelers' Circular and Horological Review, January 19, 1927, p. 52

55. Wide Pictorial Bracelet with Stylized Flower
Circa 1925

Rubies, sapphires, diamonds, emeralds, and platinum
Signed by Tiffany & Co.

Flower Brooch
1920s
Diamonds, amethysts, enamel, and platinum
Signed by J.E. Caldwell & Co.

56. Manufacturing Jewelers' Designs for Pictorial Bracelets of Oriental Inspiration
Circa 1925

First design:
By Oscar Heyman & Bros.

Last three designs:
By William Scheer, Inc.

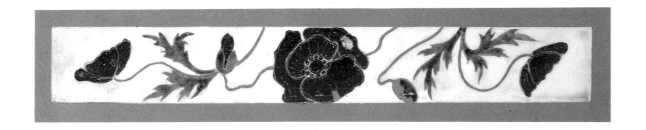

with a high intrinsic value, American retailing and manufacturing jewelers tended to translate these designs into jewels with precious rather than semiprecious stones; they favored specially cut diamonds, rubies, sapphires, and emeralds.

The desire for linear and geometric designs manifest in Cubist art was also influencing diamond cutting now. The first new fancy cuts were introduced to America from Europe in the early 1920s. They became increasingly popular and, by 1927, were being employed for entire jewels. The new cuts were termed: kite, hexagon, square, half-emerald cut, lozenge, pentagon (called bullet when narrow).

The Merger of Black, Starr & Frost–Gorham, Inc.

Black, Starr & Frost and the retail store of the Gorham Company at Fifth Avenue and Forty-seventh Street merged during America's financial boom in January, 1929, to combine their clients for their mutual benefit. The resulting firm was Black, Starr & Frost–Gorham, Inc., which was housed in the newly designed premises of Black, Starr & Frost at the corner of Fifth Avenue and Forty-eighth Street. The business was associated with Spaulding–Gorham, Inc. of Michigan Avenue, Chicago, which had a branch at 23 Rue de la Paix in Paris.

1920s' Sport and Daytime Jewelry

Although Europeans attempted to promote themselves as authorities in all matters pertaining to dress and jewelry, certain Americans also were ready to speak out on these issues. Florenz Ziegfeld, famous for the beauty of his showgirls, wrote a series of syndicated articles in the New York American in 1925. The impresario addressed the question of how to choose jewels appropriate for the time of day and manner of dress, and how to enhance a woman's attributes; one article was entitled "How Jewels Decorate Women's Personality."[7]

By mid-decade, both the buying and the wearing of jewels were topics of interest in even the smallest American towns, and these subjects were being covered by the national press.

The automobile had been transforming life in the United States. Most motor cars were open vehicles. Riding in them or driving them was considered a sport. As a result, automobile riding, tennis, and golf were linked together in people's minds and seemed

57. Vanity and Lipstick Case with Islamic Motif
1920s

Yellow gold and enamel
Signed by Black, Starr & Frost

58. Enamel Vanity Cases
1920s
Signed by Black, Starr & Frost

Yellow gold, enamel, mother-of-pearl and shell, hardstone, diamonds, and platinum

Yellow gold, enamel, mother-of-pearl and shell, hardstone, jade, diamonds, and platinum

Yellow gold, enamel, mother-of-pearl and shell, hardstone, diamonds, and platinum

The inlaid plaques on the top and bottom cases are initialed "M" for the Russian craftsman Vladimir Makovsky, who worked in Paris for leading French jewelry houses. Makovsky's technique, which combines mother-of-pearl, shell, or hardstone with metal, recalls Japanese and Chinese work.

Opposite, clockwise from top left:

59. Mystery Clock in the Oriental Style
1931

Platinum, yellow gold, onyx, lapis
lazuli, diamonds, emeralds, mother-
of-pearl, and rock crystal
Signed by Black, Starr & Frost

The hands of a mystery clock are set
on separate crystal disks, which are
grooved and attached to a driving
mechanism concealed in the design.
As a result, the hands seem to move
mysteriously. Illustrated in *Vogue*,
December 1, 1931, p. 45.

60. Gentleman's Watch
1920s

Designed and manufactured by
Verger Frères, Paris
Yellow gold, enamel, rock crystal, and
ivory
Signed and retailed by Feagans
and Co.

Feagans and Co., a Los Angeles
jewelry retail firm, was founded in the
19th century

**61. Table Clocks Incorporating
Oriental Motifs**
Designed and manufactured by
Verger Freres, Paris

1929
Onyx, coral, platinum, diamonds,
enamel, lacquer, yellow gold, and
mother-of-pearl
Signed and retailed by Greenleaf
& Crosby

1927
Onyx, enamel, purpurine, lacquer,
silver, yellow gold, diamonds, and
lapis lazuli
Signed and retailed by Black, Starr &
Frost

**62. Table Clock in a Stylized Skyscraper
Design**
1929
(this page)

Designed and manufactured by
Verger Frères, Paris
Agate, onyx, lapis lazuli, yellow gold,
sapphires, lacquer, platinum, and
diamonds
Signed and retailed by Brock & Co.

Brock & Co., a Los Angeles jewelry
retail firm, was founded in the 19th
century.

to require appropriate ornament—or sport jewelry as it was called then. The wristwatch of the 1920s succeeded the ornate watch bracelets and chatelaine watches of the mid-1910s. The wristwatch's miniaturized movement was a novelty and treated like a gem. The result was so appealing that there was a demand for thin companion bracelets. To satisfy this demand, jewelers created what would be the most popular jewel of the decade—the flexible box bracelet. Later, when worn in quantity, it would be called a new form of multiple elegance.

The geometric jewelry of the 1920s, and in particular the enormously successful box bracelets, had to be machined during manufacture. Since the turn of the century, larger jewelry workshops in America had employed machinists to make tools and dies for stamping operations. This eliminated tedious handwork and irregular results in the creation of standardized elements: stone settings, box bracelet sections, and mechanical fittings such as pins, catches, earring backs, and ring shanks. The box bracelet, in particular, benefited from the labor-saving methods that had been popularized over the last twenty-five years: the manufacture of such multiple-unit jewels could not have been done profitably by hand.

In the jeweler's panoply, these successful watch and bracelet combinations were accompanied by new vanity cases (this American term soon replaced the French term *poudrier*, or compact) and smoking accessories for women, designed with the motorist or sport participant in mind. In a Marcus & Co. advertisement of 1927, some of the American woman's favorite jewels were listed and described admiringly, "Her lorgnette, her vanity case, her lingerie clasps, acquire new significance. Her wristwatch is a little miracle. Her lipstick case is a work of art."[8]

Americans were pursuing the sporting life in Newport, Palm Beach, Deauville, Biarritz, Monte Carlo, and on the Riviera. They took cars, yachts, trains, oceanliners, and later, planes to reach their destinations, which called for daytime jewelry and costumes appropriate to the pageantry of arrival.

The resort season in Florida was called "Our Southern Season" by jewelers. Whether jewels were bought in New York or Palm Beach at this period, they were as impressive as those worn in Deauville or Cannes—and as important to the annual sales of jewelers.

America had developed its own resort jewelry, with sport and leisure motifs translated into precious materials. William Scheer's game fish in platinum, pavé diamonds, and enamel were an example of this style. Marlins, sailfish, wahoos, bonefish, and giant pompanos were made into charms, brooches, or appliqués for cigarette boxes, lighters, objets d'art, and jewelry. (The members of the Scheer family

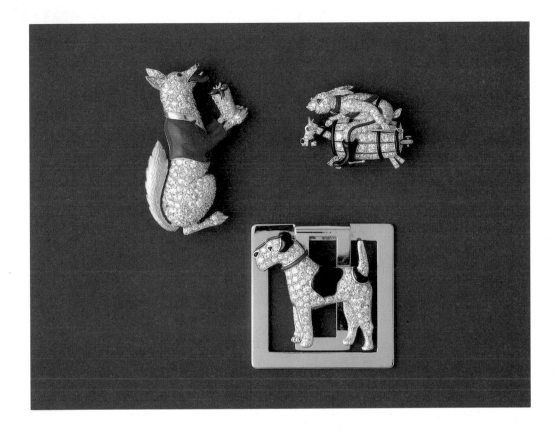

Clockwise from top left:

63. Two Comic Brooches
By Raymond C. Yard

1920s
Fox as master of hounds, holding a
mint julep
Diamonds, enamel, and platinum

1931
Rabbit jockey riding a beer barrel with
a horse's head
Diamond, enamel, rubies, and
platinum

Dog Money Clip
With inscribed date, "1930"

Diamonds, enamel, onyx, and
platinum
Signed by Udall & Ballou

64. Watch Bracelet
1920s

Diamonds and platinum
Signed by Tiffany & Co.

65. Three Bangles
1920s

Diamonds, sapphires, rubies,
yellow gold, and platinum
Signed by Bailey, Banks & Biddle

were fishing enthusiasts and are reputed to have had examples of their catch packed in ice and sent to their designers at the factory in New York.)

Cartier, New York produced some coconut palms in pavé diamonds with baguette-diamond fronds and briolette-diamond coconuts. These were themes that continued to be popular through the 1930s.

Russian Taste

After World War I, fashion correspondents flocked back to Paris. What they found was an austere postwar style epitomized by the simple, sleeveless frock with stark, geometric lines. The severity of these clothes was offset by panels of embroidery, handmade by members of the Russian émigré community in Paris. These Russians were the greatest influence on dress styles of the 1920s, and they influenced jewelry styles as well.

After the Russian Revolution of 1917, Russian aristocrats arriving in Paris brought fabulous jewels with them which they exchanged at French jewelers for currency. Other Russian gems came on the market in Istanbul (formerly Constantinople), an age-old trading center with links to the Parisian jewelry industry. Parisians and Americans alike were impressed by these necklaces that had once adorned the nobility at Czar Nicholas II's court. In some instances, they acquired them; and in others, they copied the jewels.

The presence of examples of Russian court jewelry gave rise to speculation on the fate of the fabled imperial Russian treasures. American and European gem dealers sought to obtain jewels, gems, and objets d'art from the new Bolshevik government, which was badly in need of currency. They worked with Soviet jewelry agents in Paris and Berlin, and in some cases traveled to Russia in their quest for royal acquisitions.

"What will become of the crown jewels?" was the question that was inevitably asked. The movements of the jewels owned by the czar's immediate family were followed with the enthusiasm once lavished on the French crown jewels. Prince Youssoupov brought to New York a collection of the czar's jewels and objects, which was exhibited in the summer of 1924 in a showroom at 677 Fifth Avenue. Some of the jewels were later sold by Cartier, New York, notably a strand of natural black oriental pearls. (They were purchased with some fanfare by a senator's wife, Mrs. Peter Goelet Gerry).

The influence of these Russian treasures was freeing formal Western jewelry from past restraints: chains of diamonds became longer than before; emerald drops and

Clockwise from top left:

66. Table Clock with Chinoiserie Motif
1920s

Silver, lapis lazuli, and enamel
Signed by Cartier, New York

Vanity Case with Persian Motif
1927

Yellow gold, enamel, diamonds,
cabochon rubies, and platinum
Signed by Cartier, New York

67. Cigarette Case with Airplane Motif
With inscribed date, "1928"

Yellow, pink, and white gold
Signed Black, Starr & Frost

68. Vanity Case

With American folk motif
Yellow gold and enamel
Unsigned

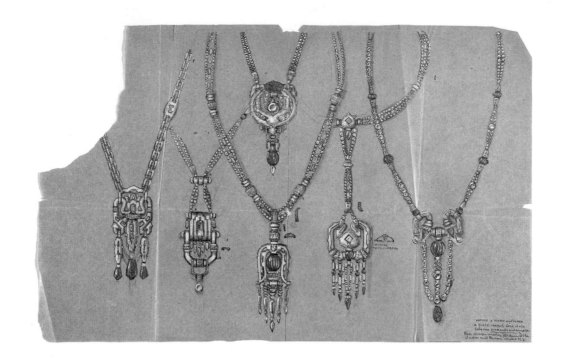

69. Designs for Emerald and Diamond Necklaces
1927

Ink and gouache on paper
By William Scheer, Inc.

70. Pendant Necklace
1925

Pearls, emeralds, diamonds, and platinum
Signed by Cartier, New York

71. Necklace

1925

Carved emeralds, diamonds, pearls,
and platinum
Central emerald motif detaches to be
worn as a brooch.
Signed by Cartier, New York

beads of astonishing size and barbaric splendor began to inspire new forms of jewelry.

The popularity of emeralds in this decade can be attributed to the combined vogue for things Russian and oriental, very much in evidence after the influx of members of the Russian aristocracy into international society. Russian royalty, in contact with the northern princely states of Mogul India because of shared trade routes, had always had the same veneration as the maharajahs for huge, colorful stones and rich ornament. The Russians had been the great buyers of large gems through the centuries, and now they were teaching the West about opulence.

Emeralds

The scarcity of fine emeralds first became evident as the gem became more fashionable. From the middle of the sixteenth century onward, western Europe obtained the majority of its emeralds from Colombia and the rest from the Orient and Russia. Prior to World War I, the output of the emerald mines at Muzo in Colombia had been consistent, but with the outbreak of hostilities in Europe, production and distribution ceased. During and after the war, with traditional sources cut off or in dispute, crown jewels once again provided the needed quality stones.

Mrs. Edith Rockefeller McCormick bought a Russian emerald-and-diamond necklace from Cartier, Paris, which she had remounted. When she wore it in Chicago to the envy of all her friends, American newspapers covered the event and publicized the necklace widely: emeralds were as popular in America as they were in Paris.

End of the Decade

In 1923, Pierre Cartier had made a statement to the American press: "It is interesting to note," he said, "that the amount of jewels owned by the citizens of any country is in direct ratio of [sic.] the business prosperity of that country.

"For example, after the French Revolution, the nobles and royalists who had owned most of the valuable jewels in France lost their wealth and were forced to leave the country and sell their most valued possessions. The émigrés turned naturally to England and Russia, which were in the full blood of prosperity at that time, and sold their jewels there.

"Today neither England nor Russia is so prosperous and these same stones which once graced the court of Versailles in the time of Louis XVI are being brought to

America and sold to those whose fortunes have been accumulating through the prosperity of this nation. The finest jewels in the world have found their way here. None but the best would serve, for the American people insist on the finest in precious stones just as they do in art and music.

"Pearls," Cartier said, "seemingly were the most popular jewels with American women at the moment and a well-matched pearl necklace, one of the most coveted of possessions."

"Precious stones most in demand, in addition to pearls," he added, "are diamonds and emeralds. There has been, however, a strong revival in the purchase of rubies, which are extremely popular at present. The purchases of gems and jewels today is coming to be regarded more and more in the light of an investment. This tendency has been given a decided impetus as a result of the revolutionary changes in Austria and Russia.

"Possessors of jewels in those countries found that they had an international medium of exchange in their possession, which preserved its full value, even though the currency into which other wealth must be converted might have depreciated so tremendously in value as to be practically worthless. Many Russians now living outside that country are existing entirely on the proceeds of the sale of their jewels."[9]

Many of these points continued to be valid at the end of the decade. Seemingly limitless financial resources and supplies of precious materials at this time, as well as the newly established link with the fine and decorative arts promoted by museums and exhibitions, and the support of enthusiastic patrons had made this a memorable decade for jewelers.

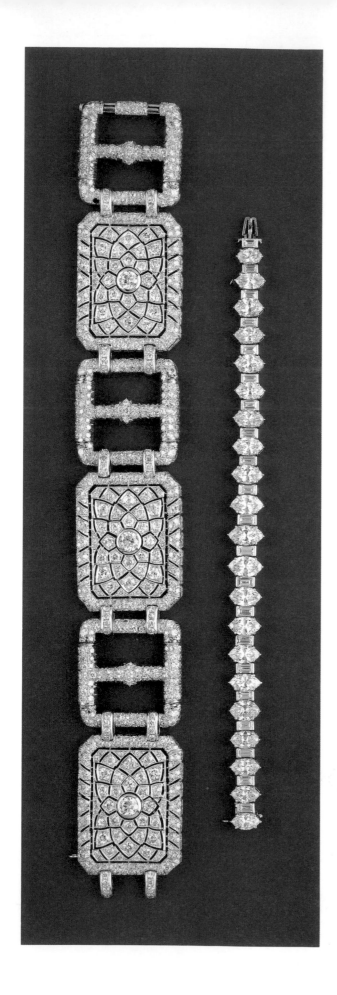

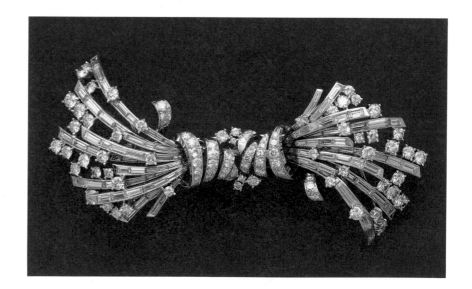

Chapter Seven

From the Depression to World War II

William Scheer, Inc.

By 1929, William Scheer was the largest manufacturing jeweler in America, making over 50 percent of the fine jewelry in the country. The clients of this firm were the most prosperous retail jewelers of the period: Marcus & Co., Tiffany & Co., Black, Starr & Frost, Raymond C. Yard, Inc., Udall & Ballou, Harry Winston, Cartier, New York, Spaulding & Co., C. D. Peacock, Shreve, Crump & Low, Galt & Bros. in Washington, D.C., Mermod, Jaccard & King, Brock & Co., Inc. in Los Angeles, Shreve & Co., Inc., in San Francisco, Greenleaf & Crosby, Grogan in Pittsburgh, Linz Brothers in Texas, to name only a few.

It is very difficult to imagine the quantity and quality of jewelry that this firm produced. There were platinum line bracelets in various widths, utilizing all the new fancy-cut diamonds: long, elaborate diamond necklaces suspending carved emeralds or detachable diamond plaques; shorter necklaces including carved Indian rubies, sapphires, or emeralds; and endless varieties of brooches incorporating intricate lapidary work. The firm also made beautiful ornate watches, ranging from gentlemen's rock-crystal-and-diamond watches to ladies' baguette-diamond watch bracelets and brooches. Scheer's created jeweled accessories: ornate handbag frames, cigarette holders, and elaborate vanity and cigarette cases after original French designs. The work of this firm was as contemporary and chic as the best work of the French manufacturing jewelers in this period. The majority of William Scheer's work was unsigned, however, and when signed, only with the retailer's name.

William Scheer and Van Cleef & Arpels

William Scheer was the agent in America for the Parisian firm Van Cleef & Arpels: when Americans bought from Van Cleef & Arpels in France, the pieces were shipped unmounted to New York in order to avoid the 80 percent duty on finished jewelry;

Clockwise from left:

72. Wide Bracelet
Early 1930s

Diamonds and platinum
Unsigned

Bracelet
Late 1950s

Diamonds and platinum
By Harry Winston

73. Clip Brooch
Early 1930s

Diamonds and platinum
Signed by Raymond C. Yard

74. Clip Brooch
Late 1930s

Diamonds and platinum
Unsigned

William Scheer assembled and remounted the jewelry, did any necessary custom work, and delivered the finished pieces to Van Cleef & Arpels's clients. This part of William Scheer's business was so large that the American and Parisian firms entered into an agreement whereby the designs of Van Cleef & Arpels would be manufactured in New York by William Scheer and retailed by that firm under the name of Van Cleef & Arpels at 671 Fifth Avenue (the establishment opened its doors on October 1, 1929).

William Scheer, Greenleaf & Crosby, and Van Cleef & Arpels

Beginning in 1926, the year Florida's real estate started losing value and two monumental hurricanes destroyed Miami's tourist business, William Scheer had extended long-term credit to the Florida firm Greenleaf & Crosby. The indebtedness of Greenleaf & Crosby was compounded in 1929 by the failure of the New York stock market. William Scheer paid off the other creditors of the Florida firm and assumed possession of the company.

On November 1, 1930, an advertisement in *Town and Country* listed Van Cleef & Arpels and Greenleaf & Crosby together at 671 Fifth Avenue, with branches in Palm Beach and Miami Beach. This lasted for a short time only because of the unfvorable financial climate: Van Cleef & Arpels shortly dissolved its agreement with William Scheer and removed its name.

The Early 1930s

The worst financial and social crisis of the twentieth century ushered in the 1930s. In America in the wake of the stock market crash, more jewels changed hands than ever before. Unlike previous periods, when jewels were given up because of changing styles or wartime needs, these jewels were relinquished to buy necessities. They went to banks as the payment on loans; to pawnbrokers and auctioneers in New York and Atlantic City. They flooded in from both private clients and jewelers in distress. With this huge stock on their hands, banks sold the jewels at widely differing rates—some very low. Many of these jewels dated back to purchases of crown jewels by Americans in the second half of the nineteenth century.

European jewelers were also caught unprepared by the stock market crash of 1929, and their fortunes were intertwined with those of American jewelers in the aftermath, particularly in the matter of natural pearls. Paris had been the world buying center for the natural oriental pearls that enjoyed great popularity from 1910 onward. Many of the big American jewelers were heavily in debt to European pearl wholesalers. The Depression produced a radical devaluation of natural oceanic pearls: pearl prices fell to one-tenth of their previous value, and they were to remain low for many years. Subsequent changes in pearl-producing regions, such as the discovery of oil in the Persian Gulf, diverted the labor force from pearl diving into the oil industry, which paid higher wages. By the time financial recovery came to the world's economy, the fashion for extravagant pearl necklaces had passed, and the cultured pearl had supplanted the natural pearl because of its novelty, availability, and low price.

Having so many debts outstanding abroad, both American manufacturing and retail jewelers paid as best they could, frequently with finished jewelry. The failing economy had slowed production and sales for jewelers. The Christmas season of 1929 was not the lucrative one that had been foreseen before the October crash of the New York stock market. Many big jewelry companies were forced to lay off staff in the new year, since orders did not materialize; production was at an all-time low. Yet jewelry continued to be made, and a new style was emerging.

The geometrical, cubist, and archeological styles of the 1920s were outdated: they were associated with too many unhappy memories. Two-dimensional jewels were also out-of-date; solid expanses of gems with special lapidary work were no longer in favor nor economically feasible. Platinum and white gold, which had been the preferred metals, were being replaced too.

A broad openwork diamond bracelet that relied on empty spaces as much as on gem patterning to achieve its bold impressive look, came into prominence. In addition, the empty spaces represented a small financial saving. Diamond pendant earrings also continued to evolve, finally widening into dangling chandeliers. The plaque—a popular necklace motif—also became longer, broader, and more open; as did the diamond brooch.

In fashion there was a new emphasis on a curvaceous silhouette for women. Contemporary dress styles were long, luxurious, and very feminine, with a distinctive widening and broadening at the shoulder and neckline. The 1930s clip brooch was a very successful adaptation of the traditional brooch that relied on a pin attachment at the back: rather than piercing dress material with a pin, the clip brooch pinched or gripped the fabric with a hinged mechanism. This construction dictated the clip's placement.

It was an off-center ornament, which could be placed anywhere along the bodice. Clips were usually made in pairs that, when combined with the help of an additional mechanism, became magnificent brooches. The clip was one of the most versatile

75. Old Grand Dad Whiskey Bottle with Clock Inside
Early 1930s

Glass, metal, cork, paint, and paper
Signed by Cartier, New York

Dice Clock with Retractable Cup and Three Dice
Early 1930s

Silver gilt and enamel
Signed by Black, Starr & Frost

jewels ever invented, for the variety of ways in which the clip brooch could be worn enabled a woman to achieve manifold effects with a single jewel. As *Vogue* reported, "The jewel has become essential to the dress, too—an integral part of it. Clips are placed at the base of the shoulder-straps; at the hollow of a drapery; at the end of a back decolletage. The jewel is an architectural motif."[1]

The clip brooch was successful beyond all expectation. Admittedly people were selling their jewelry out of economic necessity, but if there was any improvement in their circumstances, they replaced the jewelry sold with multi-purpose jewels: brooches that could be separated into two clips, necklaces that could be made into bracelets; clip brooches, earrings, and even rings were the popular recovery jewels. Prohibition as well as the Depression had been curtailing entertaining in America. Nightclubs were deserted, and in their place were speakeasies run by racketeers. When Congress passed the Twenty-first Amendment repealing Prohibition on February 20, 1933, and with the first glimmer of financial recovery, the nation again became festive.

"Gold is news these days; news makes fashion, and fashion is the life of business."[2] The news in April, 1933, was that the United States was abandoning the gold standard. Governmental restrictions on hoarding gold produced an increased public awareness of the metal and a desire to own it in some legitimate form. Jewelers had been taking in yellow gold for its scrap value in the era of platinum-dominated jewelry in the 1920s, and in increasing amounts since the Depression. Now they began returning it to the market place.

Paul Flato

Certain names will always be associated with 1930s gold jewelry in America. One of them was Paul Flato, whose firm was located at 1 East Fifty-seventh Street in New York. Flato was a man about town, a much sought-after guest at parties, who had an instinct for the clever gold jewel that appealed to members of society in the 1930s. Such jewels, while not expensive, served as incentives to bring into his shop customers who went on to buy expensive jewelry as well. Flato's humor and charm found expression in a personalized "say-it-in-jewelry" style: gold boxes, pins, rings, clips, and earrings with the wearer's initials or the expression of a sentiment as their theme. Angels—or devils—on his earrings whispered in ears; boxes had telephone dials with I LOVE YOU as the numerals.

Louis Tamis of Louis Tamis & Son, manufacturers for Flato's gold objects and jewelry, remembers him as a "pleasant, mild-mannered, attractive young man"[3] who, even in very lean years, had clients waiting for his work.

A photograph of the opera and film star Lily Pons
1930s

In this portrait she is wearing a necklace by Paul Flato, with the name of her husband André Kostelanetz, and a charm bracelet with their combined initials.
(Photograph: courtesy of the Museum of Modern Art, New York)

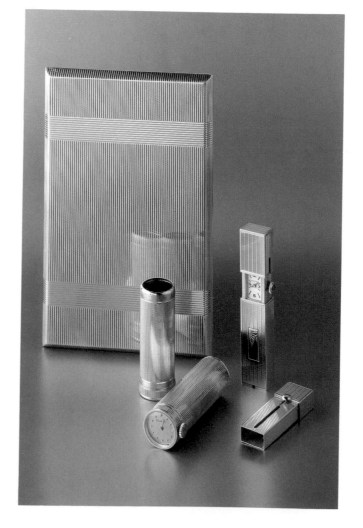

Two of Flato's clients also designed jewelry for him: Mrs. James V. Forrestal and Millicent Rogers Balcom, responsible for his "wiggly clips," jewels that moved with the motion of the wearer, and his "fat hearts," puffy heart pins, brooches, and earrings. These jewels were referred to as "whimsies." Mrs. Forrestal brought back a silver flat-link bracelet from Europe, which became the prototype for Flato's gold link bracelet, which has been popular ever since. The first identity bracelet was also a result of Flato's "say-it-in-jewelry" style.

Louis Tamis & Son

Louis B. Tamis emigrated to America from Russia in 1891. He was a master craftsman with a knowledge of how to work platinum and various colored alloys of gold. In 1905 Tamis was the foreman of Woods & Chattellier; there he worked with the man who would later be his partner, Bernard Schanfein.

Schanfein & Tamis (founded in 1909) was located on Maiden Lane originally. In 1930, after Schanfein died, Tamis reorganized his firm with his son, who was also named Louis; it became Louis Tamis & Son. One of the company's first products was a silver cigarette box with gold stripes, a process Tamis Sr. invented. Its success established the business as one of the major casemakers in the country; they produced many of the vanity cases sold during the 1920s. Whether they were enameled or inlaid with colored gold, American boxes and cases were usually executed in 14-carat gold rather than in 18-carat gold, which was commonly used in Europe. During the Depression, the firm's association with Paul Flato caused it to diversify into jewelry and novelties—pens, pencils, and money clips—all created with sophistication and wit. Louis Tamis & Son also made gold boxes for Trabert & Hoeffer, Inc.–Mauboussin.

A very popular American cigarette case was the so-called Prince of Wales Cigarette Case, originally made in September, 1924. The model (a case by Fabergé) was brought by a wealthy American to Charlton & Co. expressly so that a duplicate could be made for the Prince of Wales. Louis Tamis & Son recreated the distinctive, engine-turned case with alternating sections in green and pink gold; it was decorated with a moiré pattern on the green-gold sections and with a striped design on the pink-gold ones. The case proved so successful that the design was applied to lighters, lipstick cases, puff-powder boxes, and vanity cases as well.

Trabert & Hoeffer, Inc.–Mauboussin

In March, 1929, in one of the first advertisements of the New York firm Trabert & Hoeffer, Inc., a pair of diamond earrings said to have belonged to Catherine the

Opposite, clockwise, from top left:

79. Brooch
Mid-1930s

Pink and yellow gold, rubies,
diamonds, and platinum
Unsigned

80. Brooch
Mid-1930s

Yellow gold, carved emerald,
diamonds, platinum, rubies, and
black enamel
Signed by Cartier, New York

81. Cuff Bracelet
Mid-1930s

Platinum, diamonds, and rubies
Signed by Tiffany & Co.

82. Bracelet
Mid-1930s

Yellow gold, citrine, amethysts,
diamonds, and platinum
Signed by Trabert & Hoeffer,
Inc.–Mauboussin

Great, empress of Russia, were featured. The jewel's history was written by one of the firm's founders, R. J. Trabert. Trabert & Hoeffer, Inc. was located at 522 Fifth Avenue in the Guaranty Trust Co. Building on the corner of Forty-fourth Street. The establishment also had a branch in Paris at 58 Rue Lafayette and one in Detroit, Michigan, at 120 Madison Avenue.

On October 1, 1929, Mauboussin announced the opening of a salon at 33 East Fifty-first Street in New York. Mauboussin's timing could not have been more unfortunate: on October 29, 1929, the New York stock market collapsed. The Parisian firm was left with a large inventory in this country. Desperate to withdraw with minimum losses, Mauboussin reached an agreement with Trabert & Hoeffer, Inc. whereby the American firm would assume Mauboussin's inventory and name; the new business was called Trabert & Hoeffer, Inc.–Mauboussin.

By the early 1930s, Trabert & Hoeffer, Inc.–Mauboussin had moved its location to Park Avenue at Fifty-fifth Street and had branches in Los Angeles, Atlantic City, Miami Beach, Palm Beach, and Paris. The firm was associated with a unique line of gold jewelry which it called "Reflection—Your Personality in a Jewel."

These "Reflection" jewels were the first to implement in America the modern, European trends that had been on display at the 1931 Colonial Exposition in Paris. There the emphasis had been on yellow gold and exotic materials such as ivory, bone, lizard skin, tropical woods, and panther claws. The exotic materials did not appeal to Americans, but the yellow gold and large, colorful semiprecious stones did.

The "Reflection" jewels could not have been made without casting; they represented a successful, early application of the technology. Like the European jewels at the exposition, the "Reflection" jewels were made in 18-carat yellow gold, which was unique in America, and set with semiprecious stones (which had little value at this time).

Casting enabled Trabert & Hoeffer, Inc.–Mauboussin to fabricate jewels with standardized elements; a client could put them together any way she liked to create a jewel that fitted her personality. Previously this had been a perogative of the wealthy alone. While the pieces in this line of jewelry were not entirely handmade, they were hand-finished and cost-effective.

During the financial retrenchment of the 1930s, the "Reflection" line received great publicity; these jewels had an aura of fine, custom work at an affordable price. They were popular immediately, and by the late 1930s, the designs had been refined to such an extent that the "Reflection" jewels truly reflected their times: smooth-sided curves defined their contours instead of angles. This was indicative of the revolution in American product design that was to come.

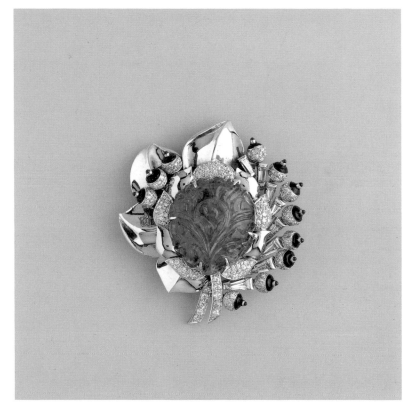

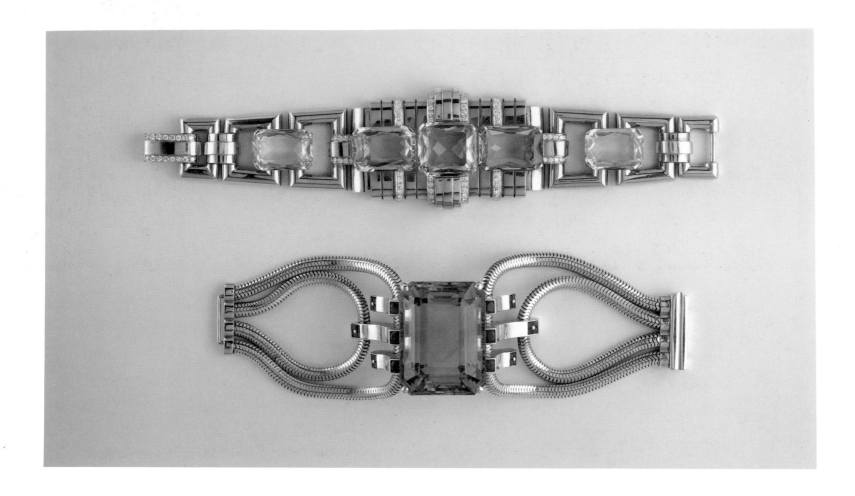

83. Bracelets
Late 1930s
Unsigned

Yellow gold, citrine, and rubies

Yellow gold, platinum, citrines, and diamonds

84. Manufacturing Jeweler's Designs for Bracelets
1930s

By Oscar Heyman & Bros., Inc.

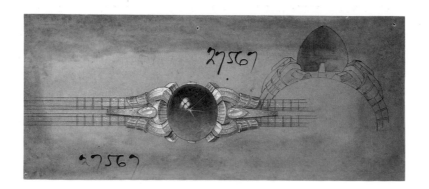

The Influence of Hollywood

A film still with Greta Garbo and Charles Boyer from Conquest
1937

In this still Greta Garbo is wearing the necklace and bracelets given by Napoleon I to Empress Marie-Louise on the birth of their son. Trabert & Hoeffer, Inc.–Mauboussin supplied this suite of antique emerald, ruby, sapphire, amethyst, topaz, diamond, and enamel jewelry for the film. These jewels were obtained from the Archduchess Immaculata of Vienna.
(Photograph: courtesy of the Museum of Modern Art, New York)

A film still from Two Faced Women, with Greta Garbo wearing Paul Flato's jewelry
1941

(Photograph: courtesy of the Museum of Modern Art, New York)

A publicity still of Jean Harlow with a star sapphire brooch
1930s

(Photograph: courtesy of the Museum of Modern Art, New York)

A publicity still of Joan Crawford wearing her star sapphire suite of jewelry
1930s

(Photograph: courtesy of the Museum of Modern Art, New York)

American jewelers had always cherished the hope that they could be innovators, but not until the mid-1930s did such a thing seem possible. The movie industry with its glamorous images came to the aid of the fashion industry. "Do American women want American clothes?" asked Adrian, designer to the stars in an article in *Harper's Bazaar*.[4] He answered positively, "Her change of viewpoint has been brought about very largely by the movies. The movies have popularized American design as nothing else could do."[5] Hollywood became the showcase of luxury and style during the 1930s, presenting contemporary dress and jewelry as well as period costumes and antique jewelry.

This brought about a revival of romantic motifs, particularly bows, flowers, sunbursts, sheaves of wheat, and shooting stars, all of sizable dimension.

The jeweler Paul Flato and his designer Fulco di Verdura (at 8657 Sunset Boulevard in Los Angeles) and Trabert & Hoeffer, Inc.–Mauboussin were designing unique and individual pieces and lending antique jewelry to wealthy society women and to Hollywood stars such as Katharine Hepburn, Greta Garbo, Merle Oberon, Joan Crawford, Marlene Dietrich, Joan Bennett, and Madeleine Carroll.

America now had its own uncrowned royalty, who took on the responsibilities of living royally. By the end of the 1930s, extraordinary jewels were very much in evidence. They were seen at parties and written about in such places as the columns of *Town and Country*; for instance the article in the November, 1937 issue on "These Disarming Women Ablaze,"[6] which recorded women wearing Empress Eugenie's pearls and emerald ring, Mary Queen of Scot's black pearls, the Youssoupov black pearls, the

85. Bracelets and Clip Brooches
Late 1930s

Sapphires, emeralds, diamonds, and platinum
By Paul Flato

The matching clips and bracelet are similar in design to the Flato jewels worn by Merle Oberon in the movie *That Uncertain Feeling*.

86. Bracelet
Late 1930s

Diamonds and platinum
By Paul Flato
Inspired by a ruby-and-diamond bracelet that belonged to Empress Josephine, consort of Napoleon I.

87. Pearl Necklace
1919–29

Perfectly matched strand of oriental
rosé-colored pearls with diamond-
and-platinum clasp
Assembled over a ten-year period;
sold by Raymond C. Yard in 1929 to
John D. Rockefeller, Jr. (Shown here
restrung.)

88. Ring

Sapphire, diamonds, and platinum
John D. Rockefeller, Jr. bought this
62-carat sapphire in India from a
maharajah in 1934. It was made into a
pendant brooch by Raymond C. Yard.
(Shown here in a modern resetting.)

Left to right, top to bottom:

89. Rose Brooch
Mid-1930s

Diamonds, rubies, and platinum
Manufactured by Oscar Heyman &
Bros., Inc.

**90. Manufacturing Jeweler's Designs for
Three Flower Brooches**
1930s

By Oscar Heyman & Bros., Inc.

91. Wax Maquette for a Brooch
1939

Depicting the Trylon and Perisphere of
the 1939 World's Fair, New York
Made by Oscar Heyman & Bros., Inc.

queen of Portugal's emeralds, the yellow diamond of Emperor Francis Joseph of Austria, among others. Still on the market were the pendant pearl earrings that had belonged to Empress Carlotta of Mexico and Cartier, New York's Russian imperial nuptial crown. Americans of high society mingled together in their attire, crown jewels, modern resettings of spectacular gems associated with famous names, and modern jewels in an elaborate, regal style.

The Flower Style

In 1936 King Edward VIII of England abdicated in order to marry the American-born divorcee Wallis Warfield Simpson, who became the Duchess of Windsor after her marriage to him. She was one of the most widely discussed and emulated women of her era and noted for her exquisite clothes and jewelry. In an American photograph, the Duchess of Windsor was shown wearing a Van Cleef & Arpels brooch composed of a spray of wild flowers in diamonds and topaz-colored sapphires.

That brooch is reputed to have launched a Flower Style in American jewelry. Important examples of antique flower jewels that came to light contributed to the popularity of this style. The beauty and wearability of the originals were revealed to Americans in the social columns of magazines and in the national press. For instance, Paul Flato supplied Mrs. Vincent Astor (a boxholder at the Metropolitan Opera) with her farewell gift to the diva Lucrezia Bori. *Harper's Bazaar* of May, 1936, reported that her gift was a "magnificent diamond brooch, three sprays of incredible 100-carat glitter and a cluster of currant leaves. Designed by the Keeper of the Crown Jewels in 1856 for the Empress Eugenie, it was always one of her favorite jewels."[7]

Influenced by the European court jewels of an earlier period, the Flower Style was a phenomenon of the High 1930s, as the period of recovery has been termed ever since. Of course, there were flowers suitable for evening wear and others for daytime wear. Evening flowers for formal wear, such as Paul Flato's rose or lilac, were made of diamonds and platinum. The formal floral jewels inspired another variety that was composed of yellow gold and less precious gems, such as Ceylon sapphires in multiple hues or semiprecious stones (amethyst, aquamarine, tourmaline, peridot, topaz, and many others). Certain manufacturing jewelers were identified with these pieces, most notably Oscar Heyman & Bros., Inc., which produced floral jewels for many firms, including Shreve & Co., Shreve, Crump & Low, Marcus & Co., Udall & Ballou, and Tiffany & Co.

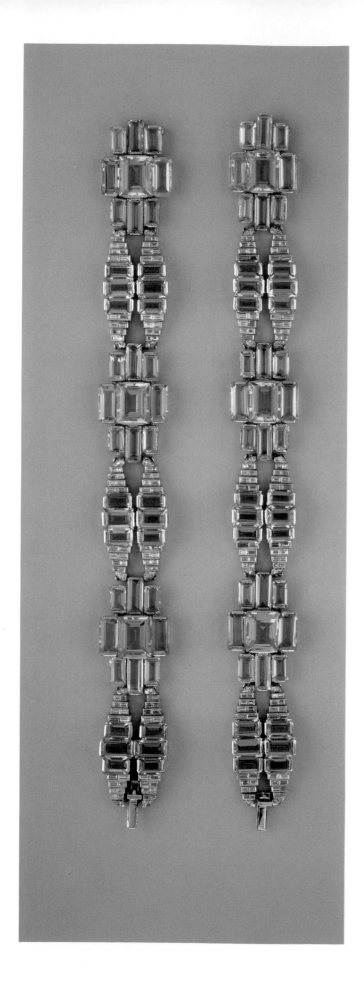

Chapter Eight

World War II

The New York World's Fair (1939)

1939 was a year of extravagance in jewelry, fostered by a wave of prosperity and also by concern for the future. Events were looming ominously once again in Europe, and assets in the form of gems and jewelry were being transferred to the United States and found a ready market there.

America was out of the Depression, and the New York World's Fair—a celebration of the world of tomorrow—naturally included the dazzling jewelry produced in New York. The focal point for jewelry at the World's Fair was the House of Jewels, the smallest building, albeit the most sumptuous. It had been contributed by five Fifth Avenue jewelers. Four of them—Tiffany & Co., Black, Starr & Frost–Gorham, Inc., Udall & Ballou, and Marcus & Co.—had roots in the nineteenth century; the fifth, Cartier, New York was an honorable latecomer, which had been established in the city since 1909. Their jewels represented the culmination of the 1930s' Style: flowers and abstract patterns of swirls, volutes, and scrolls. The jewels were conceived in gold and platinum, and enhanced with fine gems as well as with magnificent aquamarines, tourmalines, and amethysts. These jewels were architectural in effect, since the size of the principal stones and the number of subsidiary ones demanded a well thought-out substructure. The historical references that come to mind when viewing these jewels are the monuments of the Greeks and the Mayans, which had similar motifs on their facades. Set beside its 1929 counterparts, this jewelry is larger in size, showing that—lean years not withstanding—American jewelry was bigger and bolder than ever before.

Olga Tritt, Inc. in the Brazilian Pavilion

Olga Tritt was a Russian beauty who had trained as a goldsmith in her native country. She started her own jewelry firm in New York in 1910. One of her first advertisements in the 1920s featured Russian antique jewelry including black pearls, individual pearls of large size, and precious stones. Her firm was located at 730 Fifth Avenue in New York.

Left to right:

92. Matched Bracelets
Late 1930s

Aquamarines, diamonds, and platinum
Unsigned

93. Bracelet
1930s

Rubies, diamonds, and platinum
Manufactured by William Scheer, Inc.
Illustrated in *Vogue*, December 8, 1930, p. 73

94. Bracelet
1938

Aquamarines, diamonds, and platinum
Retailed by Greenleaf & Crosby
Manufactured by William Scheer, Inc.

95. Necklace

1940
(opposite)

Moonstones, sapphires, and platinum
Signed by Raymond C. Yard

96. Bird Brooches

1940
Moonstones, rubies, diamonds,
platinum, and rose gold
Signed by Marcus & Co.
Birds detach to form individual
brooches
Illustrated in a Marcus & Co.
advertisement in *Vogue*, December 1,
1940, p. 58

19th Century
Diamonds, rubies, yellow gold, and
platinum
Birds detach to form individual
brooches
In a fitted case signed by Montgomery
Bros., Los Angeles, a 19th-century
retail jeweler.

97. Two Flower Brooches

Early 1940s

Tourmalines, citrines, and platinum
Signed by Marcus & Co.

Peridots, rubies, diamonds, yellow
gold, and platinum
Unsigned

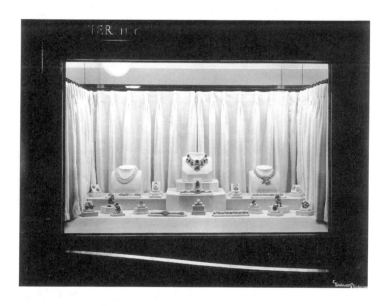

RUSSIAN ANTIQUE JEWELRY

BLACK PEARLS   ODD PEARLS (large size)
PRECIOUS STONES

OLGA TRITT
730 FIFTH AVENUE, NEW YORK

Olga Tritt was known for large jewels and for successful combinations of precious and semiprecious stones. She became an intrepid traveler in her quest for acquiring them, going to India and South America.

At the time of the World's Fair in New York, the Brazilian government asked her to create a collection utilizing the finest examples of semiprecious stones from its mines. She presented this collection in their pavilion at the 1939 World's Fair to great acclaim.

Personalized Jewelry and Objects

During the late 1930s and early 1940s, more jewelers than ever before were making custom jewels for clients. The fashion had begun in 1937 with an exhibition of Fabergé jewels and objects at the Hammer Galleries. Fabergé had obviously worked with individual patrons in mind. The results (wonderful combinations of gems, metals, hardstones, and enamels) inspired Americans with a desire for personalized precious jewelry.

A friend of the Duchess of Windsor wore a thistle by Fulco di Verdura. From Cartier, New York the duchess herself bought a series of British commemorative medals rendered in precious stones. A black-gloved hand holding a gem-set fan is reminiscent of other jewels whose owners are now unknown. A number of these precious mementos were discussed and sketched in a *Vogue* article headed, "Very Truly Theirs."[1]

The conductor André Kostelanetz gave his wife, the soprano Lily Pons, a Van Cleef & Arpels brooch for her debut in Donizetti's opera *La Fille du Régiment*; it depicted the vivandière Marie in gold, rubies, sapphires, and rose-cut diamonds. Another Van Cleef & Arpels brooch was Mrs. Gilbert Miller's diamond-and-ruby "Red Boy," inspired by the famous painting *Don Manuel Osorio* by Goya, which her father owned (later she gave the painting to the Metropolitan Museum of Art).

A black-and-white enamel piano, the cover of Ilka Chase's first book, an airplane bangle, hunting and fishing charm bracelets, or the occasional coat of arms became recognizable jewels, boxes, and cases of the era—"awards of merit"[2] for women of accomplishment. All of these ornaments, it should be noted, are representational works in miniature.

Fulco di Verdura

Fulco Santostefano della Cerda, duc di Verdura, was of noble Sicilian lineage, a superb artist who loved to paint miniatures. He had been spotted in Paris by Coco Chanel in the early 1930s and later designed the jewels and Byzantine bangles that she wore

Photographs of the display cases of the five Fifth Avenue jewelers in the House of Jewels at the 1939 World's Fair in New York:

Marcus & Co., Tiffany & Co., Cartier, New York; Black, Starr & Frost; Udall & Ballou

Advertisement for Olga Tritt

The Jewelers' Circular and Horological Review, January 10, 1929, p. 56

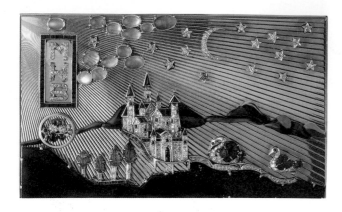

Clockwise from top left:

98. Cigarette Box with Romantic Landscape
Inscribed with date, "Christmas, 1945" and initials "MHB"

Pink, green, and yellow gold, moonstones, jade, lapis lazuli, emeralds, diamonds, rubies, sapphires, and enamel
Unsigned

99. Cuff Bracelets with Commemorative and Sentimental Charms
Early 1940s

Diamonds, sapphires, rubies, emeralds, enamel, yellow gold, and platinum
Unsigned

100. Commemorative Box and Original Design
With presentation inscription, "To my daughter Ilka with unfailing love Edna Woolman Chase April 8, 1942"

Yellow gold, lacquer, diamonds, and platinum
Signed by Paul Flato
Manufactured by Louis Tamis & Son
A gold box with the cover of Ilka Chase's first book *Past Imperfect*, given to her by her mother Edna Woolman Chase, the editor of *Vogue*.
Illustrated in *Vogue*, December 15, 1942, p. 46

Clockwise from top left:

101. Brooch and Design
1940s

Platinum, diamonds, yellow gold,
enamel, sapphires, rubies, emeralds,
and moonstones
Manufactured by Oscar Heyman &
Bros., Inc.
Design contemporary with brooch but
unsigned.

102. Royal Orb Brooch
1947

Star sapphire, emerald, yellow gold,
rubies, diamonds, and platinum

Manufactured by LaSalle for
R. Esmerian, Inc. LaSalle was a
venerable New York manufacturing
firm that was well-known in the 1920s;
it went out of business in the 1970s.
The last of a group of jewels consisting
of twelve historic English emblems,
which were purchased in 1947 by the
Duchess of Windsor from Cartier,
New York.

**103. Cigarette Box and Bracelet with
Applied Game-Fish and Animal
Charms**
1937

Yellow gold, lacquer, diamonds,
platinum, and rubies
Signed and retailed by Charlton & Co.
Manufactured by William Scheer, Inc.

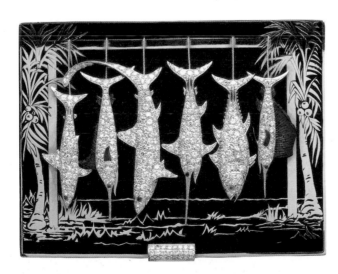

constantly. He had been Chanel's eyes and ears at parties in Paris before he went to New York to design for Paul Flato. After a couple years in America, the duke had achieved a certain celebrity of his own. He had created commemorative boxes for Flato's famous clients Cole and Linda Porter, and the box he created to commemorate Porter's musical *Red, Hot, and Blue* was acclaimed in the February 1, 1937, issue of *Vogue*. After a few years working for others, Verdura was ready to set up on his own and to create a personal style, drawing upon art history, mythology, and the life he had led in interwar Europe.

Fulco di Verdura established his firm at 712 Fifth Avenue on September 1, 1939. At that time Verdura, Inc. produced light-hearted jewels with a new whimsical look: a 6-inch kite; an umbrella, for fair weather or foul, with jeweled raindrops; and other caprices. The jewels were variously described as "dramatic," "interesting," "witty," or "personal."

Since platinum was being used in the war effort and the prices of fine gems were exorbitant, Verdura started out with jewels made of yellow gold and semiprecious stones, many of which came from refugees' jewels and proved to be of extraordinary color. Afterward his painter's eye impelled him to find stones of rare and exceptional color. In the late 1940s, Verdura purchased 100 carats of bright pink precious topaz from Russia, which had been popular in Victorian jewelry. The topaz, which had been mined in the Ural Mountains, had been sold to jewelers in London during the nineteenth century. Later Verdura incorporated this topaz into his own jewelry.

Seaman Schepps

The designs of Seaman Schepps, an American jeweler, had a lightness of heart that suited the 1930s and 1940s well. Schepps was an admirer of Suzanne Belperron (a Parisian designer for Hirz-Belperron, who created sculptural jewels with an uninhibited sense of splendor) and also of Paul Flato and Fulco di Verdura.

Since 1934, Schepps had been located in New York at 388 Madison Avenue diagonally across from the Ritz-Carlton. His jewels enhanced the dress styles of the time: brooches well-suited to the wide shoulders of contemporary dress and short necklaces for the high necklines. Schepps created a range of gold bracelets and cocktail rings that were composed of precious and large, semiprecious stones. He was a lover of the odd gem, the oriental figurine, the antique curio; he transformed them and incorporated them into jewelry, winning the patronage of Coco Chanel, Elsa Schiaparelli, the Duchess of Windsor, and Gertrude Lawrence. This demonstrates just how appealing and unique American jewelry had become.

104. Commemorative Cigarette Case for Cole Porter
1942

Yellow gold
Interior inscribed, "Something to Shout About, December, 1942."
Signed by Fulco di Verdura
Cole Porter wrote the film score and lyrics for *Something to Shout About.*

105. Commemorative Cigarette Case for Cole Porter
1939

Caricatures depict authors George S. Kauffman and Moss Hart; John Hoyt in the role of Beverly Carlton, and Monty Woolley as Sheridan Whiteside in the play *The Man Who Came to Dinner.* Engraved silver and lacquer, inlaid with yellow-gold letters
Interior inscribed, "For Cole Porter because we think you're wonderful. Moss and George."
Signed by Fulco di Verdura

Clockwise from top left:

106. Thistle Brooch
1940s

Yellow gold, canary and white
diamonds, emeralds, and platinum
By Fulco di Verdura

107. Brooch and Matching Earrings
1940

Aquamarines, diamonds, and
platinum
By Fulco di Verdura

108. Wing Brooches
1945

Aquamarines, diamonds, platinum,
and yellow gold
Signed by Fulco di Verdura

109. Heart Compact
1948

Tourmalines, aquamarines, and
yellow gold
Signed by Fulco di Verdura

Ring
1948

Kunzite, diamonds, yellow gold, and
platinum
Signed by Fulco di Verdura

110. Page of Designs
1940s–60s

By Fulco di Verdura

111. Violet Nosegay Brooch
1940

Amethysts, diamonds, emeralds,
yellow gold, and platinum
Signed by Fulco di Verdura

C1108

C1107

C1106

C1105

C1101

C1100

C1095

C1103

C1092

C1094

C1098

C-1090

C1086

C1089

C-1076

C-1087

132

112. Page of Designs
1940s–60s
(opposite)

By Fulco di Verdura

This page, clockwise from top left:

113. Wreath Ear Clips
1951

Canary and white diamonds, yellow
gold, and platinum
Signed by Fulco di Verdura

Bow Tassel Ear Clips
1950s

Precious pink topaz, diamonds,
platinum, and yellow gold
Signed by Fulco di Verdura
Manufactured by Carvin French, Inc.

114. Shell Brooch
1960

Enamel, diamonds, yellow gold, and
platinum
Signed by Fulco di Verdura
Manufactured by Carvin French, Inc.

115. Bracelet
1950

Diamonds, platinum, and yellow gold
By Fulco di Verdura

116. Turtle Statuette
1950s

Malachite, yellow gold, peridots,
coral, diamonds, sapphires, and
platinum
Signed by Fulco di Verdura

117. Suite of Gem-Set Jewelry with Compact
1948
(opposite)

Cultured pearls, rubies, sapphires, emeralds, diamonds, platinum, and yellow gold
Signed by Seaman Schepps

118. Necklace
1958

Turquoise, diamonds, yellow gold, and platinum
Signed by Seaman Schepps

119. Brooch
1960s

Rock crystal, diamonds, and platinum
Signed "PVS" for Patricia S. Vaill, daughter of Seaman Schepps

Ring
Late 1950s

Coral, diamonds, yellow gold, and platinum
Signed by Seaman Schepps

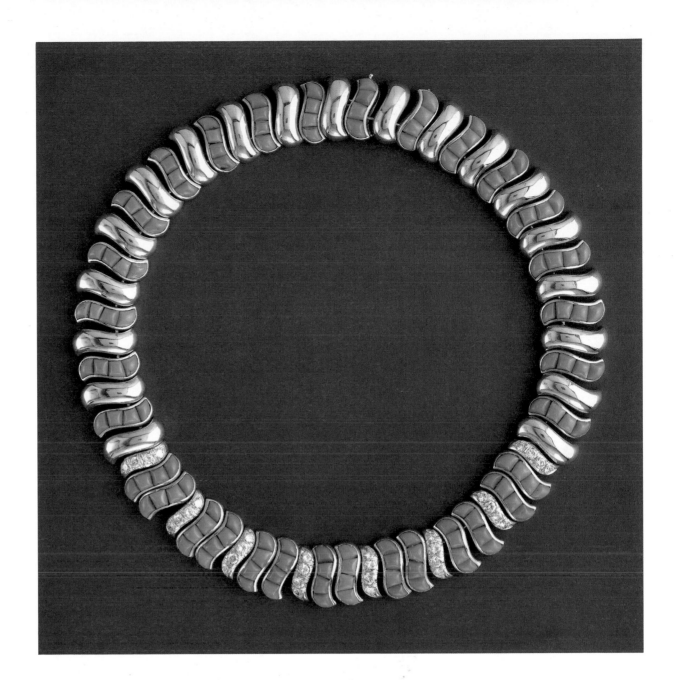

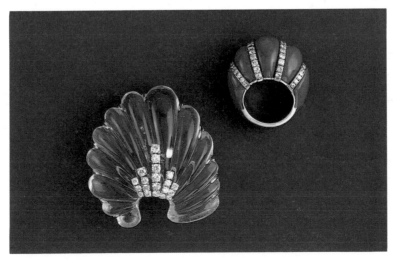

120. Miniature Birdcage
1940

Diamonds, rubies, sapphires, jade, yellow gold, and platinum
Signed by Seaman Schepps

121. Shell Earrings
1949

Turbo shells, emeralds, and yellow gold
Signed by Seaman Schepps

122. Oriental Statuette Brooch
Late 1930s

Aquamarine, tourmaline, rubies, sapphires, diamonds, yellow gold, and platinum
Signed by Seaman Schepps

Wartime Jewels

America entered the war that had broken out in Europe in 1939 after Pearl Harbor, on December 8, 1941. Curiously, the wartime style in jewelry was pictorial, fanciful, and delightful. It was a time of birds, baskets of flowers, dancers, and tranquil images—seals with flexible diamond whiskers that made patrons and jewelers alike laugh. Patriotic jewels were also popular, of course. Brisk and cheerful, these included well-appointed military figures (both male and female), a dapper Uncle Sam, and the American flag.

While most American jewelry firms concentrated on design and color (emphasized by an increased use of large semiprecious stones and yellow gold), Cartier, New York, a firm with European origins, provided an exception. In its Fifth Avenue windows, Cartier, New York exhibited magnificent precious gems—emeralds, sapphires, and rubies, enhanced with diamonds—proving that styles are passing phenomena in jewelry, while fine gems are enduring. Cartier, New York's display was indicative of the times: America was becoming the center of the gem-trading world.

Flight of the Diamond Industry

Diamond dealers and cutters were coming to New York from the diamond centers in Europe—Antwerp and Amsterdam—bringing merchandise and tools with them. When possible, they had hidden their larger tools and machinery to prevent them from falling into enemy hands. In New York, these craftsmen found a small but active European community, members of their trade who had fled during World War I. Some of those who had come to the United States in the late 1930s stayed and set up business. They soon found that only stones of high quality and larger size could be cut with profit in America. A number moved on to Puerto Rico and Cuba upon discovering that it was not profitable to cut small stones in America. They trained a new generation of diamond specialists there, for the industry in Latin and South America. Still others deposited their goods in American banks or with relatives and went back to fight, utilizing their knowledge of languages and terrain with the Allied forces. (Members of this group of émigrés were particularly valuable in Allied espionage efforts.)

European dealers in colored stones were also going to New York. The Nazi occupation of the Netherlands, Belgium, and France forced many of them to emigrate to England, Switzerland, or America. During the war, however, it had seemed that the future of fine jewelry would really be in the United States.

Emerald necklace with rectangular pendant
Late 1940s

R. Esmerian, Inc. acquired the seven matched emeralds in this necklace from the Paine Whitney family. The pendant emerald (weighing 106.45 carats) was acquired by Cartier, New York in the 1920s from Prince Youssoupov. It was reputed to be the second largest emerald in the Russian treasury, surpassed only by Catherine the Great's emerald.

Emerald necklace with pear-shaped pendant
Early 1950s

In 1952 R. Esmerian, Inc. recut the Cartier emerald into a pear shape (weighing 75.63 carats) to eliminate a major flaw. The remaining part of the rectangular gem was cut into a navette. The new necklace, with an additional matched emerald, was sold to John D. Rockefeller, Jr. in 1954.

The lavish spending on gems in the late 1930s, the fabulous presentation of jewelry at the 1939 World's Fair, the establishment of a branch of Van Cleef & Arpels in New York, and the movement within the diamond industry had ramifications that could not be ignored by anyone whose business was fine gems and jewelry. Even American jewelers realized that they were to be hosts to groups of people who would transform their businesses. Always noted for an appreciation of fine stones, American buyers would now have access to superior jewels and gems on their own soil, thanks to the inventories of the new arrivals.

Leading American retail jewelers in New York were particularly aware of the changes the fleeing Europeans were effecting in the jewelry industry. In 1939, one of them, Raymond C. Yard, an American jeweler with a clientele among the elite, asked the most prominent French wholesale-gem dealer, Raphael Esmerian, if he would consider coming to New York. Esmerian's acceptance assured Yard and other leading American jewelers of an access to stones of a quality formerly available only in Europe. Although Esmerian was the most significant colored-stone dealer to come to America, other gem dealers were also transferring their business assets to America in the uncertain times preceding and during World War II. This enabled them to move their inventories and families to safety, while continuing to do business or serving in the Allied forces.

Alternate Trade Routes

Traditionally American gem buyers had traveled to Paris and London to procure the finest stones from European and Far Eastern gem merchants. World War II put an end to buying in Europe, and Nazi expansion curtailed the international gem trade. The representatives of the oriental gem-producing countries went home; the Japanese held the areas of Indochina, Thailand, and Burma famous for high-quality sapphires and the blue star sapphires popularized in America by the movie star Joan Crawford. Spinels, zircons, garnets, topazes, and jade also came from these areas and had previously been exported through India.

America's jewelers met the challenge by setting up a direct trade link with the Far East, which the Trans-Pacific Airmail made possible; it flew packets of gemstones into the United States. After the bombing of Pearl Harbor in 1941, this trade route no longer went across the Pacific Ocean. Gems from the Orient went via East Africa, Sierra Leone, or Liberia across the Atlantic Ocean to Brazil and then up to the United States.

123. American Flag Bow Brooch and Designs
1940

Rubies, sapphires, diamonds, and platinum
Signed by Cartier, New York
Designs contemporary with brooch by William Scheer, Inc.

124. American Theme Brooches
1940s
Signed by Cartier, New York

Patriotic star-shaped flag brooch
Yellow gold, lacquer, diamonds, and spinel
Illustrated in *Vogue*, December 1, 1940, p. 95

Two American Indian bird brooches
Yellow gold
With presentation inscription on one, "To Pudgeon From Wm Boyd 12 25 47" (Bill Boyd, internationally famous as the American cowboy, Hopalong Cassidy)

Indian chief brooch
Yellow gold, lacquer, turquoise, and diamonds

Brazil was important for another reason at this time. The majority of semiprecious stones for the jewelry industry had always been cut in Germany at Idar-Oberstein, which was no longer trading or producing. During World War I a handful of German cutters from this community had fled to Brazil, eventually training some of the native population in their craft. During World War II, these cutters supplied American jewelers with the necessary aquamarines, precious topaz, amethysts, tourmalines, and other cut semiprecious stones.

Theoretically emeralds too should have been coming along this trade route from South America into America, since one of their principal sources was Colombia. However, due to internal strife, the government-controlled mines had not been operating since 1938, and few new emeralds were reaching the markets in New York. Fine emeralds of 2 carats or more were coming out of private collections, crown jewels, and the stocks of the European and American jewelers who had been buying large, valuable colored stones from the Orient and Russia since the end of World War I.

Therefore, America was not lacking in gems for the duration of the war. This influx of gemstones transformed New York into a great repository for fine stones, whether or not they were sold there at the time.

Precious Metals During World War II

For the extent of the war, the creation of platinum jewelry was prohibited by the American government, and anyone holding platinum in any form had to report it monthly—platinum was once again needed for munitions. White gold, the alternative employed during the last war, had become associated with bold, imaginative but less expensive jewelry; consequently it held little allure for the wealthiest members of the buying public.

Palladium, one of the platinum group of metals, was put forward as an alternative. Palladium has remained an unhappy memory for fine jewelers. It was difficult to solder efficiently, and applying heat to it produced an unattractive, purplish coat of oxidation that was hard to remove. Palladium was used only as a substitute for platinum; once platinum became available again, jewelers abandoned it with relief.

Casting

Although casting was not applied to every part of a jewel, it was so revolutionary a technique that it influenced the look of all jewelry in this period and changed the nature of the industry forever.

The ancient art of lost-wax casting had been adapted and made viable as a production technology in the early part of the twentieth century by a practicing American dentist, Dr. William Taggart. The pioneer in American casting technology and equipment was the Kerr Manufacturing Co., which was founded in Michigan near Detroit in 1891 by two brothers, Robert and John Kerr. They developed and produced a gas-fired furnace for the production of porcelain dental crowns and bridges. As gold casting became more important in modern dentistry, the company worked with dentists to develop better methods and materials for casting gold inlays. By the 1930s the Kerrs were collaborating with jewelers because they perceived a new market, supplying advice, tools, and equipment. Their contribution to jewelry was equal to that of Sam W. Hoke who had developed the platinum-welding torch in 1912.

In the modern method of wax casting, a wax shape is made of an object and placed within a stainless steel cylinder with a removable rubber bottom. The cylinder is filled with a creamy, liquid form of heat-resisting plaster, called investment, which quickly hardens. The rubber bottom is then detached, and the cylinder is put into a kiln, or "burnout oven," to expose the opening to the heat. The wax shape melts and evaporates. At the same time chemical changes occur that prepare the plaster mold to receive the metal in the space left by the wax. Finally molten metal is forced into the cavity using centrifugal force, steam pressure, or simple gravity.

European jewelers also benefited from the fact that their American counterparts adopted this technological innovation. It is said that Francois Verger of the venerable French manufacturing firm of the same name went back to Paris after World War II carrying a centrifugal casting machine, because it was not yet available in France.

Rubber Molds—The Art of Multiples

The final chapter in the story of modern casting was the discovery of the technology leading to the development of the two-part, flexible rubber mold. In 1839 Charles Goodyear discovered the process of vulcanizing rubber: through the addition of sulphur compounds and the application of heat and pressure, raw rubber can be changed into a harder, stronger, more flexible and elastic material.

Just under a century later, this knowledge was applied by jewelers to make today's rubber molds. During World War II, casting was also employed in the war effort to produce radar parts. Because of the large scale of this production, the techniques involved were refined even further.

Chapter Nine

Van Cleef & Arpels in New York

Van Cleef & Arpels Stays On

The "long Armistice" that had preceded World War II came to an end in September, 1939. Immediately afterward, an event that would change and enrich American jewelry for the next quarter of a century took place: Van Cleef & Arpels, which had been exhibiting in the French Pavilion at the 1939 World's Fair, decided to stay in New York and opened premises at 744 Fifth Avenue. To Americans this action was perhaps the most visible example of the changes taking place in the age-old European jewelry business.

One of the most celebrated feats of Van Cleef & Arpels was producing the invisible setting, an innovation of the 1920s. The emphasis on stones and cutting in that decade had accelerated the search for a concealed setting, which had been a jeweler's dream since the nineteenth century.

Langlois, a member of the Van Cleef & Arpels workshop in Paris, patented the first setting of this type in 1929, according to Claude Arpels. It had not been perfected, however. As a result of the stock market crash, it did not come to America until the mid-1930s.

The invisible setting was a new technique; it can be considered one of the great contributions of the twentieth-century goldsmith to the history of jewelry. It was introduced in America in the October, 1936 issue of *Vogue* on a flower jewel made by Van Cleef & Arpels, Paris (which had taken out a patent for the technique in the firm's name in 1933).

The setting presents an array of gems with no metal mounts visible. The preferred gems—sapphires, rubies, and upon occasion, emeralds—must be perfectly matched or their color will not be uniform. Many gems are discarded in the process of cutting and mounting. The gems are square-cut and grooved on the back along parallel sides, custom-cut to fit snugly against each other. One by one, they are put on to concealed tracks, which hold them in place.

125. Earrings with Invisible Setting
1941

Rubies, diamonds, and platinum
Signed and retailed by Van Cleef &
Arpels, New York
Manufactured by Bury & Rubel

126. Leaf Brooch with Invisible Setting
1950s

Rubies, diamonds, yellow gold, and
platinum
Signed and retailed by Van Cleef &
Arpels, New York
Signed and manufactured by Oscar
Heyman & Bros., Inc.

Because of the specialized cutting involved, these gems can never be remounted in other settings, and the value of the jewel is that of the finished object. Only the most sophisticated workshops were capable of selecting gems for this setting, carrying out the custom-cutting, producing the mount, and assembling the various parts. The setting was still so novel in 1936 that it was variously labeled as "mysterious," "concealed," "hidden," or "invisible." The name itself was never patented, although Van Cleef & Arpels continues to be identified with the finest examples.

Although many techniques had to be mastered to complete the various steps involved in making the invisible setting, American workshops were soon capable of producing their own versions. The fact that the invisible setting could be adapted to both abstract and representational motifs insured its popularity in the coming years.

Due to its expertise in machining, Oscar Heyman & Bros., Inc. was among the first American manufacturing jewelers to work with this setting. Augusto Iberti, a smaller workshop located on Fifth Avenue and Fifteenth Street, was also able to produce a limited number of invisible settings.

Jewels with invisible settings were popularized in America by the heiress Barbara Hutton, who saw a rare example with emeralds—a ring—at Charlton & Co. in New York and ordered one for herself. Emeralds, very fragile gems, were the most difficult precious stones to mount in this fashion.

During World War II, Van Cleef & Arpels in New York kept the tradition of fine jewelry alive in America—fortunately; for with the austerity of the war years and general financial vicissitudes, four important New York firms shut their doors: Charlton & Co., Udall & Ballou, Marcus & Co., and Paul Flato. A fifth, E. M. Gattle, went out of business at the end of the 1940s.

John Rubel Co.

Van Cleef & Arpels's Parisian manufacturing jeweler, John Rubel Co., followed the firm to New York, emigrating via South America. In New York the two firms again began to work together, utilizing the talents of the same designer, Maurice Duvalet. Duvalet was a Frenchman who had lived in America since the end of World War I; previously he had worked for Charlton & Co. A rare individual and a superb draftsman, Duvalet brought "chic to everything he touched."[1]

His most significant jewel dates from the earliest days of his association with these two firms, a ballerina brooch in rose-cut diamonds. One version of the inspiration behind this jewel says that Robert Rubel, John's brother and a partner in his firm, who was watching flamenco dancers at a cafe in Greenwich Village, sketched the first dancer on the menu. Another version ascribes the series of ballerina brooches to Louis Arpels, the son of the French founder of Van Cleef & Arpels, who loved classical ballet and opera. Duvalet designed the Van Cleef & Arpels ballerina brooches in rose-cut diamonds. The stones used were from Spanish crown jewels which fleeing loyalists had taken to Mexico; afterward they were sold at auctions in New York.

The first diamond ballerina brooch represented Maria Camargo as she appeared in the eighteenth-century painting by Nicolas Lancret that Andrew Mellon gave to the National Gallery of Art in Washington, D.C., in the late 1930s. By abandoning the hooped dress and heeled slippers traditional for a ballerina, Camargo had created as much of a sensation as Diaghilev's star Anna Pavlova. That Russian dancer is depicted in another ballerina brooch in a characteristic pose based on a photograph of her taken in 1910, during her first appearance in America: Pavlova is about to drop into "the most charming curtsy ever seen in the Metropolitan . . .".[2]

These brooches were jewels that embodied longing: they looked back to the activities of the wealthy in peacetime—ballet, opera, and museum exhibitions. They were also frankly representational and at first competed with the 1939 World's Fair jewels, which suddenly seemed large, splashy, and outmoded in comparison. Styles were changing.

The association between Van Cleef & Arpels and John Rubel Co. was dissolved in 1943. John Rubel Co. moved to 777 Fifth Avenue in the Savoy Plaza and had branches in Paris and London

Up to 1947, when it closed, the firm received favorable publicity, for its jewels were very innovative. The Rubels, a French family of Romanian descent, had been acclimating to the New World and looking to American popular culture for suitable jewelry themes. Very early they discovered the innovative work of Walt Disney in the movie *Fantasia* (which premiered in New York on November 13, 1940). This movie inspired a folio of designs as well as John Rubel Co.'s first advertisement: a rendering of "The Graceful Three, The Dancing Flowers," the silhouettes of which bear a startling resemblance to those of *Fantasia*. The folio included other dancing flowers, a dazzling sequence of fairies with platinum bodies and rose-cut diamond wings, and a graceful Pegasus. These creations, as well as the "Rockettes" of Radio City Music Hall took their place among jewels designed as French cancan dancers, Spanish flamenco dancers, and Louis XV dancers doing the minuet. This firm delighted in themes with movement.

The Rubel line of jewels was not limited to the famous dancer brooches. The two brothers John and Robert were also intrigued by flowers. They executed camellias, passion flowers, dahlias, and "undersea flowers" in their own combinations of bright

127. Ballerina Brooches and Designs
Early 1940s
(opposite, top to bottom)

Designed by Maurice Duvalet
Signed and retailed by Van Cleef &
Arpels, New York
Manufactured by John Rubel Co.

Back of brooch depicting Maria
Camargo (an 18th-century French
ballerina) after the painting by Nicolas
Lancret in the National Gallery of Art,
Washington, D.C.
Rubies, emeralds, diamonds, yellow
gold, and platinum

Depicting Maria Camargo
Rubies, emeralds, diamonds, and
platinum

Ballerina in profile, with design
Rubies, emeralds, diamonds, and
platinum

Depicting Anna Pavlova (the 20th-
century Russian ballerina)
Emeralds, diamonds, and platinum

Depicting Anna Pavlova, with design
Rubies, emeralds, diamonds, and
platinum
Illustrated in Van Cleef & Arpels
advertisement, *Vogue*, March 15,
1944, p. 4

This page, clockwise from top left:

128. Dancing Flower Brooch with Designs
Early 1940s

Yellow gold, rubies, sapphires, and
diamonds
By John Rubel Co.

129. Ballerina Brooch
Early 1940s

Turquoise, rubies, yellow gold, and
diamonds
By Van Cleef & Arpels, New York

130. Cupid Brooch with Design
Early 1940s

Diamonds, rubies, emeralds, yellow
gold, and platinum
By John Rubel Co.

131. Cupid Brooch
Early 1940s

Designed by Maurice Duvalet
Diamonds and platinum
Signed by Van Cleef & Arpels,
New York

132. Designs
Early·1940s
By John Rubel Co.
(clockwise, from left)

Pegasus Brooch

"Wings of Victory" Brooch
Illustrated in Van Cleef & Arpels
advertisement, *Vogue*, December,
1944, p. 2. The design for this
brooch originated in 1940, when John Rubel
Co. and Van Cleef & Arpels were still
associated.

"Minuet" Brooch
Illustrated in Neiman-Marcus
advertisement, *Town and Country*,
November, 1945, p. 74

Rockettes Brooch
Illustrated in John Rubel Co.
advertisement, *Vogue*, April 1, 1946,
p. 138

133. Abstract Bird Brooch
1941

Designed by Maurice Duvalet
Citrine, diamond, and yellow gold
Signed by Van Cleef & Arpels,
New York

134. Two Bird Brooches
Mid-1940s

Designed by Maurice Duvalet
Sapphires, rubies, diamonds, yellow
gold, and platinum
Signed by Van Cleef & Arpels,
New York

135. Cartoon Jewelry
Early 1940s
(top to bottom)

Bracelet
Depicting characters from the 1939
animated film *Pinocchio*
Yellow gold and enamel
Signed by Cartier, New York and Walt
Disney Productions

Bracelet
Depicting characters from Walt
Disney's series of films *Silly
Symphonies*
Yellow gold and enamel
Unsigned

Two charms
Depicting Mickey Mouse and
Minnie Mouse
Yellow gold and enamel
Unsigned

136. Brooch
Late 1950s

Diamonds and platinum
Signed by Van Cleef & Arpels, New
York

137. Lionhead Brooch
1960s

Diamonds, emeralds, and yellow gold
Signed by Van Cleef & Arpels,
New York

138. Floral Necklace
Late 1950s

Diamonds and platinum
Signed by Van Cleef & Arpels, New
York

139. Necklace

Emeralds, diamonds, and yellow gold
Signed by Van Cleef & Arpels,
New York

Antique Indian Bracelet
17th Century

Yellow gold, enamel, diamonds,
and rubies
Unsigned

Both the antique Indian bracelet and
the emerald beads were obtained by
Claude Arpels in India in the 1950s.

151

gems; they especially favored turquoises, rubies, and diamonds—the combination of which was very new. Even their simplest jewelry was sculptural. This firm was responsible for the popularity of the large, cocktail-style domed ring with accompanying earrings.

The New Look

By the fall of 1944, Allied troops had liberated Paris. The Van Cleef & Arpels advertisement in the December *Vogue* of that year showed a fairy from *Fantasia* in rose-cut diamonds; she was renamed the Wings of Victory and seemed to hold her wand over the Parisian jewelry establishment as the lights came back on along the Place Vendôme.

Clothes in the initial postwar years were not too exciting. It was left to imaginative jewels to enliven what was, at best, pretty ordinary—the "uncluttered" look of 1945.

In 1947 Christian Dior launched the "New Look" in Paris. The wide skirts, opulent material, and plunging necklines took people's breath away on both sides of the Atlantic. The message was obvious: the world was ready for luxury once again.

The exceedingly low and flattering decolletages of formal gowns made necklaces the favored jewel at this period. Increasingly magnificent diamond necklaces were produced. The most popular were made by Van Cleef & Arpels, New York. That house was working in an updated pre-World War I diamond style, utilizing larger diamonds and taking advantage of innovations in modern goldsmithing and platinumsmithing. This firm presented America with court jewelry that incorporated scrolls, ribbons, flowers, festoons, and garlands worked out in marquise, circular-cut, and pear-shaped diamonds of superior quality.

The 1950s have been characterized as the Age of Affluence in America. National incomes rose; the gross national product increased at an astonishing rate, and America was soon producing one-half of the world's goods. In the boom, Americans once more looked to Europe for their couture fashions, but they shopped for their jewelry in New York. The diamond-and-platinum jewelry of the early 1950s was superseded by a more polychromatic style that was the result of a highly publicized gem-buying trip to India by Claude Arpels, grandson of the firm's founder and a nephew of Louis Arpels.

Indian Style Necklace
1965

Pearls, diamonds, and emeralds
Signed by Van Cleef & Arpels, New
York

Left to right:

Antique Indian Necklace
Bought in India by Claude Arpels
in the 1950s

Indian Style Necklace
1960
Yellow, blue, and pink sapphires
and diamonds
Signed by Van Cleef & Arpels,
New York

Claude Arpels in India

The Orient had always been a source of colored gems for the West. By traveling to India at a time when maharajahs were eager to exchange gems for currency, Claude Arpels opened the door to influences from India in American jewelry. Before long, brilliantly colored sapphires, emeralds, and rubies from India were transforming the initial all-white styles of the postwar era. Claude Arpels's delight in the Far East and its treasures was infectious, and though others had traveled there with similar intent, the Van Cleef & Arpels jewels were the best in the new idiom.

By the end of the 1950s, large fine gems were being lavishly utilized in jewelry to produce a truly exotic effect and the all-diamond necklace had given way to an even more opulent-looking necklace, made up of colored gems. The effect was dazzling.

The continuous change and political turmoil in the Far East was bringing fabulous gems to the West, not only from India but also from Cambodia, Pakistan, Burma, Nepal, and Tibet. Rubies, sapphires, emeralds, and diamonds had great appeal for Americans, who associated them with the mysterious East and readily accepted the styles resulting from the availability of these gems.

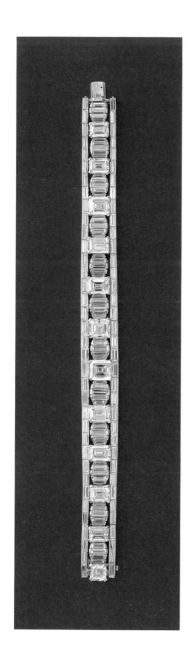

Chapter Ten

Harry Winston, Inc.

Harry Winston, Jewelry Broker

In 1932, Harry Winston opened a retail-jewelry business in New York, incorporated under his own name, at 527 Fifth Avenue. Through the 1930s Winston was variously described in newspapers and periodicals as a jewelry broker, a diamond importer, and a jeweler. He had become known in the 1920s for his ability to resell entire estates quickly, dispensing with the inconvenience of middlemen, and realizing a substantial profit for banks and trustees. Winston bought important estates and obtained some of the well-publicized gems of the period: the estate of Rebecca Stoddard (1925), the estate of Arabella Huntington, widow of the railroad magnate Collis P. Huntington (1926); the 36-carat diamond that had belonged to Elenore Elverson, wife of the owner and publisher of the *Philadelphia Inquirer* (1930); and the "Lucky" Baldwin ruby (1930), which he resold to Black, Starr & Frost–Gorham, Inc. a month later. During the Depression, Winston's special talents became even more sought after.

The Jonker Diamond

Harry Winston's taste in jewelry was formed by some of the most costly and dazzling examples of the goldsmith's art, which passed through his hands. He preferred beautiful gems arranged in lyrical clusters without the heavy metal settings and the pavé-diamond surrounds of previous eras. Winston respected the platinum technology of America and the lapidary skills of certain Americans. When he decided to enter the arena of modern jewelry retailing, he became a heroic figure almost immediately, due to his courage and daring. The firm of Harry Winston, Inc. had a simple but appropriate motto: "Rare Jewels of the World." In 1934 Harry Winston acquired the seventh largest rough diamond in the world—the Jonker Diamond—in London, a coup on the level of his first acquisitions.

Winston took the diamond to America to have it cut, an extraordinary step in the

140. Line Bracelet
1948

Diamonds and platinum
By Harry Winston

141. Necklace and Bracelet
1960s

Diamonds and platinum
By Harry Winston
After World War II, the marquise and pear-shaped diamond cuts were preferred over the rectangular and baguette cuts.

Photograph of Shirley Temple holding the uncut Jonker Diamond
1935

(Photograph: courtesy of Harry Winston, Inc.)

1930s. The Jonker Diamond, of South African origin, was the first of the world's great diamonds to be cut in the United States. After eight and a half months of careful study, Lazare Kaplan and his son Leo (64 Fulton Street, New York) began work.

The cleaving of the Jonker Diamond became a national event that was covered in newsreels, radio broadcasts, and newspapers. At the time, an American periodical stated, "no gem in the world's history has won greater fame or done more to increase the public love and appreciation for diamonds."[1] Harry Winston expressed the hope that the largest of the twelve diamonds would be bought by a philanthropist and donated as a national treasure to one of the famous museums in the United States. He made plans to exhibit some of the Jonker stones at the Metropolitan Museum of Art or at the American Museum of Natural History, and at select jewelry stores across the country: Brock & Co., Inc., Los Angeles; Shreve & Co., Inc., San Francisco; and others.

Harry Winston wanted the twelve stones obtained to have the finest modern proportions. He was prepared to sacrifice weight to obtain maximum brilliance—a brave decision at a time when historic diamonds such as the Cullinan, the Excelsior, and the Jubilee in the British Royal Collection had been cut for maximum yield. With this single stone, Winston enabled America to triumph over traditional European diamond-cutting centers; he also established the desirability of the modern brilliant cut, rendering the older diamond cuts obsolete.

Winston ushered in a bright modern look in diamond jewelry that would later become a hallmark of his style. Then he acquired the Varga (726.60 carats, rough), which had been found in Brazil and was sold in Antwerp; it was cut into thirty-nine stones. His next acquisition, the Liberator (155 carats, rough), came from Venezuela and was cut into four stones.

The Hope Diamond and "The Court of Jewels" Exhibit

In 1949 Harry Winston purchased the entire jewelry collection of Evalyn Walsh McLean (approximately seventy-three pieces), which included the Hope Diamond—an oval blue diamond weighing 45.52 carats. The McLeans had originally purchased the Hope Diamond at Cartier, Paris in 1911, and its presence in America was indicative of where the world's finest gemstones were to be found in the postwar era: European dealers were now traveling to America to buy gems.

Harry Winston, Inc.'s collection of important stones and crown jewels had become so large and impressive by this time that Winston organized an exhibit at the Rockefeller Center Forum, "The Court of Jewels." It opened on November 23, 1949, as

Texan women modeling historic and modern necklaces from Harry Winston's "The Court of Jewels" exhibit

San Antonio, 1952

a part of a benefit for the United Hospital Fund; the author Ilka Chase wrote the program notes.

This exhibit contained the Hope Diamond, the largest of the twelve Jonker stones (weighing 126 carats), the 94.8-carat Star of the East from the McLean estate, an emerald necklace that had belonged to the Earl of Dudley, the so-called Spanish Inquisition emerald-and-diamond necklace, a 60-carat emerald-cut diamond ring that had been owned by Mabel Boll, the renowned American "diamond queen," a necklace with two pear-shaped Indore diamonds (reputed to be the largest, perfectly matched twin diamonds in the world), a large Golconda diamond ring from the McLean estate, called the Idol's Eye; and a 72-carat Golconda diamond, which had belonged to May Bonfils Stanton of Denver. (Harry Winston later donated some of these jewels to the Smithsonian Institute, Washington, D.C.)

"The Court of Jewels" exhibit traveled to Winston-Salem, Dallas, and San Antonio. At each stop, it was greeted with enthusiasm and publicized in the local newspapers. As one of Harry Winston's associates later put it, "He turned America's liking for diamonds into a passion."[2]

142. Mexican Landscape
1947

White and fancy-colored diamonds,
emeralds, rubies, sapphires, jade,
yellow gold, and platinum
Manufactured by LaSalle for
R. Esmerian, Inc.

Chapter Eleven

Texas and the West

Julius Cohen

In 1955 Julius Cohen opened his jewelry salon at 17 East Fifty-third Street in New York, next to the Stork Club. The son of the eldest Heyman sister, he had gone to work in his uncles' firm, Oscar Heyman & Bros., Inc. in 1929. While traveling and selling for that firm during the Depression, Cohen opened new markets in the developing regions of the southern and western United States, making many friends in the process.

Cohen was the first to persuade Stanley Marcus of Neiman-Marcus to sell fine jewelry at Neiman-Marcus in Texas. In 1942 Cohen joined Harry Winston, Inc. and traveled with "The Court of Jewels" exhibit to Winston-Salem, Dallas, and San Antonio. By the time Julius Cohen decided to open his own firm—called Julius Cohen—in 1955, he had experienced the growing appreciation for fine jewelry across America at first hand; he was also acquainted with American taste from coast to coast.

From the beginning, Cohen wanted to produce well-designed and well-executed jewels with fine stones. Although his salon and workshop were in New York, much of his business was conducted in the homes of clients and friends, who came to depend on Cohen for jewelry tailored to their specific tastes and needs. Julius Cohen created personal jewels for special occasions, as well as classic jewels with lasting intrinsic value.

Neiman-Marcus

In the late 1930s the management of Neiman-Marcus department store in Dallas asked Chapin Marcus (no relation) of Marcus & Co. to come out of retirement to open a jewelry department in the store. Marcus was joined by Dudley Ramsden of Trabert & Hoeffer, Inc.-Mauboussin. Both men had been eminent in the New York jewelry

143. Necklace
Early 1967

Peridots, diamonds, and yellow gold
Signed by Julius Cohen

144. Phoenix Necklace
Early 1958

Diamonds, emeralds, and yellow gold
Signed by Julius Cohen
Bird detaches to form a brooch or to
perch in a sculpted, gold tree

145. Topiary Brooch
1980

Natural black pearls, fancy-colored
and white diamonds, yellow gold, and
platinum
Signed by Julius Cohen

146. Bracelet and Brooch
1980s

Fancy-colored and white diamonds
and yellow gold
Signed by Julius Cohen

147. Suite of Necklace, Bracelet, and Ring
1971
(opposite)

Star rubies and sapphires,
chrysoberyl, cat's-eyes, diamonds,
and platinum
Manufactured by George Peyrot, Inc.
for R. Esmerian, Inc.
George Peyrot, who came to New
York from Paris in 1926, established a
small workshop that manufactured
jewelry for Charlton & Co., Harry
Winston, Inc., and John Rubel Co. The
firm incorporated in 1947, becoming
George Peyrot, Inc.

148. Necklace and Bracelet
1948

Sapphires, rubies, diamonds,
platinum, and yellow gold
Manufactured by LaSalle for
R. Esmerian, Inc.

149. Necklace and Bracelet
1976
(opposite)

Sapphires, canary and white
diamonds, platinum, and yellow gold
Manufactured by Carvin French, Inc.
for R. Esmerian, Inc.

This page:

150. Two Flexible Gem-Set Bracelets
1960s

Diamonds, rubies, sapphires,
emeralds, and platinum
Manufactured by Carvin French, Inc.
for R. Esmerian, Inc.

Sapphires, diamonds, emeralds, and
platinum
Manufactured by Vors & Pujol, Inc. for
R. Esmerian, Inc.
Vors & Pujol, Inc. grew out of the
original Cartier workshop, American
Artworks (1909–41), which was
located in the Cartier building.

151. Earrings
1966
(left)

Diamonds, turquoise, and platinum
Manufactured by Carvin French, Inc.
for R. Esmerian, Inc.

152. Earrings
1966
(right)

Diamonds, turquoise, and platinum
Manufactured by Vors & Pujol, Inc. for
R. Esmerian, Inc.

153. Four-Leaf Clover Earrings
1961
(below)

Diamonds and platinum
Manufactured by Carvin French, Inc.
for R. Esmerian, Inc.

establishment and their move to Texas was an indication of an important, new jewelry market opening up there.

Wealth had been accumulating steadily in Texas since the early part of the century. Cotton barons, wild-catters in the oil strikes of the late 1910s and early 1930s, and wartime profiteers had all added to the state's growth. Each successive generation had turned to Neiman-Marcus for its luxuries and had been supplied with the finest. Now, the presence of two New York jewelers was an assurance that the same high standard would apply to jewelry.

In the early 1940s Neiman-Marcus was an emporium for Texans and other Americans and Europeans who spent their holidays in Mexico instead of Europe. The store was constantly filled with eager shoppers happy to buy jewelry, furs, and dresses in Dallas, rather than in New York. By the 1950s Texans were eager patrons of fine jewelers, and their tastes were influencing styles. Texans no longer needed to shop in New York or Europe.

Dudley Ramsden epitomized the international jeweler who had participated in the development of the great styles of the 1930s and 1940s and was well prepared to direct his resources toward the creation of a new style. His association with New York jewelers assured him access to the finest gems in the world, and the wealth of his Texan clients enabled Ramsden and the colored-stone dealer Raphael Esmerian to come up with unusual gem combinations for jewelry such as a necklace, bracelet, and ring made of diamonds, star rubies, star sapphires, and chrysoberyls.

Texans embraced this new style, recognizing the quality of the gems at once, and realizing that jewelry like this was not available anywhere else in the world. To their satisfaction, however, it could be worn anywhere in the world.

William Ruser

William Ruser and his wife Pauline opened Ruser on Rodeo Drive in Los Angeles in 1947. Ruser had his roots in the previous era. As a young man he had worked for Trabert & Hoeffer, Inc.-Mauboussin in Atlantic City, New Jersey, and he had managed its Los Angeles branch in the late 1930s. By the 1950s, the firm of Ruser was employing a staff of forty, including twenty-two journeymen jewelers, to keep up with the demand for Ruser's sculpted gold work which included butterflies, birds, fish, swans, and flowers. One of the most memorable of the Ruser jewels belonged to the actress Loretta Young—a swan with a baroque pearl as its body.

154. Ring
1958

Diamonds, emeralds, yellow gold, and platinum
Signed by Cartier, New York

155. Flower Brooch

Fancy-colored diamonds and platinum
By Harry Winston

Ring
1984

Fancy-colored diamonds and platinum
Unsigned

156. Branch Brooch
1950s

Yellow gold, opals, demantoid garnets, and fancy-colored diamonds
Signed by Wedderien

Clockwise from left:

157. Bracelet
1953

Sapphires, diamonds, and platinum
Manufactured by William Scheer, Inc.
(Photograph: courtesy of Sotheby's)

158. Bracelet
Late 1950s

Rubies, diamonds, and platinum
Unsigned

159. Bracelet
Late 1950s

Diamonds and platinum
Unsigned
(Triangular-cut diamond panel later
addition)

Clockwise from top:

160. Earrings
1950s

Sapphires, diamonds, and platinum
Unsigned

161. Narcissus Brooch
1957

Sapphires, ruby, diamonds, and
platinum
Manufactured by J. Mehrlust for
R. Esmerian, Inc.

162. Poppy Brooch
1959

Rubies, diamonds, and platinum
Manufactured by J. Mehrlust for
R. Esmerian, Inc.

163. Whimsical Brooch
1950s

Depicting a frog at the edge of a
pond
Gold, moonstone, coral, jade, pearls,
and fancy-colored diamonds
Signed by Wedderien

164. Grape Brooch
1968

Natural black pearls, canary and
white diamonds, platinum, and yellow
gold
Manufactured by Carvin French, Inc.
for R. Esmerian, Inc.

Parrot Brooch
1954

Ruby, sapphires, emeralds, diamonds,
platinum, and yellow gold
Retailed by Raymond C. Yard Inc.
Manufactured by J. Mehrlust for
R. Esmerian, Inc.

Donkey and Cart
1972

Rubies, sapphires, emeralds,
diamonds, lapis lazuli, citrine, yellow
gold, and silver
Manufactured by Carvin French, Inc.
for R. Esmerian, Inc.

165. Two Brooches
1970s

Depicting a sailboat and a bird

Diamonds, sapphires, rubies, yellow
gold, and platinum
Designed by Oscar Heyman & Bros.,
Inc.

The New Patrons

The years after World War II afforded increased leisure time to many Americans. Jewelers took advantage of the country's growing fascination with nature, love of travel, photography, *National Geographic* spreads, television, and film documentaries. There was an explosion of color in jewelry, and nature once again provided new themes for the designs.

Clients' tastes were changing. Affluent middle-class Americans across the United States joined the ranks of the jewelry-buying rich. Fashion in jewelry was gravitating toward work in yellow gold. Connoisseurs of jewelry, knowledgeable about what was new and good in this field, now wore the colorful combinations of yellow gold with semiprecious and precious gems, even on the most formal of occasions.

Chapter Twelve

The 1960s

The Kennedy Years

The early 1960s were stimulating years for imaginative jewelry designers. President John F. Kennedy, his wife Jacqueline, and their friends and associates at the White House, set a trend in style that was both sophisticated and artistic. Adornment in the Kennedy era was youthful and lively. The fact that America's First Lady was young and beautiful made fashion even more exciting for the public. Gowns worn at parties were photographed and discussed, contributing to the renown of European and American couturiers and of the jewelers who were accessorizing their clothes.

The most splendid and well-publicized jewelry was made by two firms that had risen to prominence in the 1950s: Van Cleef & Arpels, New York and Harry Winston, Inc.

From Van Cleef & Arpels came a collection entitled "Jewels Facing East." By now jewelers did not hesitate to combine rubies, sapphires, and emeralds in large, domed clusters. Such jewels were linked, as a matter of course, to Claude Arpels, who had lost neither his momentum nor his enthusiasm.

Harry Winston, for his part, continued to produce impressive diamond jewels, often adding a scroll or garland of rubies or some other colored gems. Although Winston's jewels varied from season to season, his vision transcended fashion. His house was identified with a sumptuous diamond style that he had continuously refined since the late 1940s. Winston had invented a light platinum setting in his workshop, said to have been inspired by the wirework of a Christmas wreath. This setting, which was the envy of New York jewelers, was suitable for mounting any stone and left Winston free to concentrate on his main love—gems.

Tiffany & Co. and Cartier, New York, which chose what appealed to them from the two preceding, preeminent styles, also produced jewels that reflected the magnificence of the 1960s as well as the sheer enjoyment of formal entertaining that was rapidly spreading across the country.

166. Necklace
1960

Yellow sapphires, diamonds, turquoise, yellow gold, and platinum
Signed by Jean Schlumberger

David Webb, Inc.

During this period, when Jacqueline Kennedy was seeking imaginative gifts for diplomatic purposes, she contacted the New York jeweler David Webb, for Webb had won the respect of the White House circle. His firm (established in the late 1940s with Nina Silberstein as business partner) was initially located in New York's jewelry district at Forty-seventh Street. By the 1950s it had moved to 6 West Fifty-seventh Street, upstairs and wholesaled imaginative jewelry to Bergdorf Goodman, Bonwit Teller, and private clients. In 1963 David Webb, Inc. opened a salon at 7 East Fifty-seventh Street.

Webb looked to the ornaments of other, earlier civilizations (mainly Greece, Rome, Mesopotamia, Russia, and India) for his inspiration. His gold work was reminiscent of that of the Mediterranean world and the Mayan culture of Central America. Webb admired the sculptural finesse of Peter Carl Fabergé's jewels and his imaginative combinations of Russian semiprecious stones. Webb delighted in native stones too, and in what has since been called the "wrong family of gems"[1]—baroque pearls and stones notable for their irregular color and odd shapes, frequently taken from estate jewels. Webb had studied the eighteenth-century enameled jewelry of eastern India, and his enameled bangles owed a debt to the designs of Jaipur.

Webb made a series of objects in native American materials, inspired by American themes, as state gifts: for Premier Fanfani of Italy, a paperweight of Arizona malachite; for King Hassan of Morocco, an American eagle in gold holding a citrine; and for Chancellor Adenauer of West Germany, American iron pyrites mounted in gold.

David Webb, Inc.'s work is bold and well-defined. Webb used his huge library of beautifully illustrated modern art books for reference and went to museum exhibitions frequently. The result of all of these images came out in the firm's jewelry.

The amazing success of another line of jewelry by David Webb, his "enamel jungle" of the 1960s, was reported in *Vogue*, "The big cats here are riding the crest of a wave—the return of enamel with its molten pure color brilliance—in jewelry like a fantastic bestiary."[2]

The popularity of David Webb's animals brought fame back to a towering jewelry innovator of the recent past, Cartier's Madame Jeanne Toussaint, who had joined Cartier, Paris in the 1910s and had become famous for her panthers, serpents of the Nile, little ladybugs, and turtles. David Webb himself acknowledged the endurance of her work. Speaking of his animals, he said, "It's completely Toussaint's influence, of course—she is the inspiration of us all."[3]

167. Suite of Jewelry
1970s

Rock crystal, diamonds, yellow gold,
and platinum
Signed by David Webb

Clockwise from left:

168. Feline Bracelet
1960s

Yellow gold, enamel, emeralds, diamonds, and platinum
Signed by David Webb

169. Frogs: Cuff Links, Ring, and Brooches
1960s

Yellow gold, enamel, diamonds, rubies, and platinum
Signed by David Webb

170. Brooch
1960s

Yellow gold, enamel, diamonds, and platinum
Signed by David Webb

The Animal Kingdom

As the 1960s progressed, there was an increasing demand for whimsical jewels, and everyone started producing their own versions. The story goes that Claude Arpels, spotting the door knocker of the Italian consulate, thought up the famous lionhead line of jewelry. Launching it, Van Cleef & Arpels, New York created its own animal style.

The bright and colorful daytime jewels of the 1960s inspired *Vogue* and *Harper's Bazaar* to outdo each other in photographic tableaux; cologne cascading over a lily pad was enhanced by the presence of three of David Webb, Inc.'s green enamel frogs; nail polish looked better on a hand with a Chinese dog bracelet by Van Cleef & Arpels. The results delighted the public.

By the mid-1960s, precious jewelry was being worn with abandon. Hands with a ring on every finger and two on the index finger; arms adorned with two cuffs, two bracelets, and a rope of beads—the bulk and color of this style created a very different look from that of the styles in which diamonds had predominated. *Vogue* called this style "Scheherazaderie"[4] after the beautiful, oriental storyteller of the *Thousand and One Nights*.

Customers were buying from numerous jewelry houses, and they were wearing jewels by different designers together. The traditional arrangement of one jeweler-one client also seemed to be changing.

Chapter Thirteen

Tiffany & Co. and Bulgari, New York

Jean Schlumberger and Nicolas Bongard

171. Two Bird Brooches
1940s

Enamel, rubies, sapphires, amethysts, aquamarines, emeralds, and yellow gold
Signed by Jean Schlumberger
The bird on the left was illustrated in Vogue, December 15, 1941, p. 56.

172. Animal Brooches
Signed by Jean Schlumberger
1963
Parrot
Enamel, rubies, turquoise, emerald, and yellow gold

1967
Elephant
Enamel, spinels, diamonds, turquoise, yellow gold, and platinum

Jean Schlumberger started out in Paris with Elsa Schiaparelli, for whom he created fanciful buttons and whimsical costume jewelry. By 1939 he was designing dazzling fine jewelry for a select circle of international clients.

Nicolas Bongard, a nephew of the fashion designer Paul Poiret, had worked for his uncle the French jeweler René Boivin and for the Parisian jewelry firm Lacloche Frères. In the early 1940s, when Bongard was designing buttons in New York, he met Schlumberger, who was now designing jewelry there. The two decided to pool their talents and to go into business together in America. They started out at 745 Fifth Avenue and, after a break in their careers serving with the Free French, they reopened their business at 21 East Sixty-third Street in 1947. The collaboration was successful from the start: Jean Schlumberger was already known as a designer and had a following; Bongard worked effectively behind the scenes, promoting the name of Schlumberger.

A sensitive artist and lover of nature, Schlumberger was soon designing a range of enchanting jewelry and objects that derived their inspiration from the world of nature. His jewels were imaginative recordings of rare aspects of nature, hidden to all but the keen, artistic eye; these he transformed into yellow gold, varicolored gems, and enamel. Schlumberger's work consisted of sea urchin boxes with gold barnacles; the early perpetual-motion clips—"cosmic snowflakes," seablooms, stars, and flowers.

Walter Hoving and Tiffany & Co.

In 1955, Tiffany & Co. passed out of the control of the family's heirs. Walter Hoving of the Hoving Corporation was responsible for the audacious takeover; under his management Tiffany & Co. prepared to become competitive again.

173. Islamic Style Box
   1960s

   Yellow gold, rubies, sapphires, and
   diamonds
   Signed by Louis Féron

174. Shell Clock
   1960s

   Yellow gold
   Signed by Jean Schlumberger, Tiffany
   & Co.

175. Flower Brooch
1957

Diamonds, platinum, and yellow gold
Signed by Jean Schlumberger

Bouquet Brooch
1964

Peridot, spinels, colored sapphires,
diamonds, yellow gold, and platinum
Signed by Jean Schlumberger

176. Three Brooches
Signed by Jean Schlumberger
(clockwise)

1967
Pine cone
Tourmalines, diamonds, yellow gold,
and platinum

1958
Conch Shell
Diamonds, rubies, yellow gold, and
platinum

1957
Pineapple
Sapphires, emerald, and yellow gold

177. Sea Bird Brooch
1968

Diamonds, ruby, enamel, platinum,
and yellow gold
Signed by Jean Schlumberger

178. Vine Necklace
1986

Diamonds, yellow gold, and platinum
Signed by Jean Schlumberger

In the same year, Hoving approached Jean Schlumberger and Nicolas Bongard with the proposal that they move to Tiffany & Co. to provide a challenge to the styles of the most important jewelry houses. The two men were thrilled at the idea. Whereas previously they had had to work on a limited budget, producing only one out of every ten of their designs, they could now anticipate producing all of them. Schlumberger and Bongard would continue to manage their business in New York in the new premises at Tiffany & Co., and they would own their branch in Paris, which was not associated with Tiffany & Co. It took a year to organize the arrangement. In 1956 the Schlumberger Department at Tiffany & Co. opened on the mezzanine, with its own private elevator.

Although the Kennedy years were brief, their effect on jewelry was far-reaching. The decorative arts were beginning to be regarded with a respect that extended to jewelry as well. When a retrospective of Jean Schlumberger's work, "20 Years of Jewels and Objets d'Art," was organized in November, 1961, for the benefit of the Newport Preservation Society, the First Lady attended. She could view jewels and objects that had been made for many of her friends, for example Mrs. Paul Mellon.

Schlumberger's work offered the public another alternative to the all-diamond style. The reasons for this were varied; among them, Schlumberger's objection to the impersonality of that style.

As an artist, he had his own thoughts on color in jewelry. Using Tiffany & Co.'s abundant supplies, Schlumberger mixed rubies with amethysts and peridots, and yellow with blue sapphires; the result was a different palette that achieved a new type of beauty. Schlumberger continued to use yellow gold, even in his more formal pieces; and although he is identified with yellow gold, he used platinum on occasion to set off a gem or combinations of gems when he felt the result would be more appealing.

Schlumberger's work for Tiffany & Co. continued to be based on the imaginative, lyrical, and romantic aspects of nature, heraldry, and art history. Those who were acquainted with the wit and charm of his earlier creations for Elsa Schiaparelli consider his Tiffany & Co. jewels a natural development of his style.

In this period, Schlumberger's work provided the creative spark at Tiffany & Co., assuring that the venerable firm would attract highly visible clients and the coverage in periodicals that was becoming increasingly important (Diana Vreeland was the head of *Vogue*, and Nancy White of *Harper's Bazaar*). For Tiffany & Co. was in danger of becoming entrenched in its own conservative traditions: 1-carat diamond engagement rings, circle pins, and the wedding registry. Walter Hoving sought to remedy this by hiring the first well-known American designer for Tiffany & Co., the gifted Donald Claflin, who had formerly worked for David Webb, Inc.

Donald Claflin

When Donald Claflin began to work for Tiffany & Co. in 1965, his work was receiving acclaim from a new, younger generation of jewelry buyers. He reacted to the changing market by experimenting with unusual materials, using them in unique combinations in fine jewelry. Working closely with his workshop in New York, Claflin was the first to design brooches, bracelets, rings, necklaces, and earrings with inlaid hardstones. These pieces were reminiscent of the 1920s' clocks and objects made by Verger Frères in Paris. Claflin was responsible for many original combinations in jewelry: one of his bracelets incorporated woven Moroccan leather, gold, and stones; he also brought ivory and exotic hardwoods back into fashion. Claflin was responsible for what many have called a revolution. Whereas artistic American jewelry had traditionally included semiprecious stones, he conceived his Tiffany & Co. jewelry with only the finest of gems, materials, and workmanship; these had become available to him through his connection the venerable firm of Tiffany.

Claflin's work is large, colorful, and very attractive. He enticed the women across the country who had never given up their respect for Tiffany & Co. to become more adventurous and to adopt a bolder statement in jewelry as part of their dress and new body language. Thanks to Schlumberger and Claflin, Tiffany & Co. led the way toward a modern, sophisticated style in jewelry, and the rest of America was willing to follow.

Donald Claflin had won a following of enthusiastic young clients through his interpretations of the much-loved characters in children's literature: the walrus from *The Walrus and the Carpenter*, the frog-he-would a-wooing-go, and that all-American hero, the mouse Stuart Little, about to set sail on Central Park Lake. Imaginative, informal jewels like these provided an outlet for the creativity of jewelers and an opportunity for the wearers to express their individuality.

The Changing Market

In the 1970s, Tiffany & Co. observed that its clientele was changing: the tailored, working woman was coming to the fore; more women than ever before were buying their own jewelry and accessories. The most popular jewelry now tended to be in the medium price range.

This was a period of widely publicized name designers in America, who were changing their collections seasonally and capitalizing on the modern woman's desire to be up-to-date. The board of directors at Tiffany & Co. demanded that sales per square foot increase, and the company looked with interest at successful, contempo-

179. Sailor Mouse Brooch
1966

Designed by Donald Claflin
Diamonds, platinum, enamel, and
yellow gold
Retailed by Tiffany & Co.
Manufactured by Carvin French, Inc.
Depicting Stuart Little, the hero of
Stuart Little, a children's classic by
E. B. White, published in 1945 by
Harper & Row. (Photograph: courtesy
of Christie's)

180. Disk Brooch
1970s

Designed by Donald Claflin
Ivory, cabochon emerald, diamonds,
rubies, sapphires, turquoise, and
yellow gold
Signed by Tiffany & Co.
Manufactured by Carvin French, Inc.

181. Sea Dragon Brooch
1968

Designed by Donald Claflin
Diamonds, emeralds, rubies, enamel,
yellow gold, and platinum
Retailed by Tiffany & Co.
Manufactured by Carvin French, Inc.
(Photograph: courtesy of Christie's)

rary enterprises such as Bloomingdale's. The jewelry firm decided to develop in-house name designers with whom women could identify. This designer phenomenon called for the creation of seasonal collections in jewelry linked to a shrewd awareness of current styles and colors in fashion. Both of the new designers Tiffany & Co. hired were working women: Angela Cummings and Elsa Peretti.

Angela Cummings

Angela Cummings had come to Tiffany & Co. in 1967 as Donald Claflin's assistant; she was a trained goldsmith. Her vision of jewelry proved refreshing to women all over the United States. Cummings was inspired by the traditional arts of Japan; she experimented with materials and forms from nature, weaving leaves of yellow, red, green, gold and copper into collars evocative of autumn. Cummings was also capable of boldness, which became apparent later in her gold bracelets inlaid with semiprecious stones and mother-of-pearl.

Elsa Peretti

The Italian Elsa Peretti was a former model for the fashion designer Halston; she began designing silver jewelry in 1969 and had exhibited her work in a boutique at Bloomingdale's. Peretti had an established sense of her own style; she was highly articulate in the fashion press.

Peretti came to Tiffany & Co. in 1974; she was a true sculptress in miniature, responsible for reinstating sterling-silver jewelry in the Tiffany & Co. showcases after a hiatus of twenty-five years. Naturally she also branched out into gold jewelry with precious stones. The greater part of Peretti's work in both silver and gold (which includes beans, teardrops, and hearts) has the mysterious quality of biomorphic shapes. From her tiniest charms to her large zodiac bracelets, the jewels she executes emphasize the undulating planes and the play of light and shadow commonly associated with sculpture. As a result, each one of Peretti's jewels can be exhibited as a small, decorative object as well.

Carvin French, Inc.

Tiffany & Co. was able to make bold statements in jewelry in the late 1960s and early 1970s because they were working with a New York manufacturing jeweler that was one of the finest in the world. The principals of this firm were two Frenchmen, Serge Carponcy and André Chervin. The two men had worked together at the manufacturing jewelry firm of Louis Féron in New York and went on to found their own firm at 12 East Fifty-second Street (later at 16 East Fifty-second Street) in 1954. Their firm's name, Carvin, was an amalgamation of their two names, and "French" was added to imply European workmanship—both men, having trained in Paris, had completed the traditional French jeweler's apprenticeship.

In the late 1940s, when Paris was still suffering from the devastation of World War II, the two men felt that prospects in America would be better than anything they could expect in their native country.

On arrival in New York, they were immediately successful. There had been a swing in American manufacturing jewelers toward casting and other mass-production techniques that did not require the all-encompassing skills of master jewelers. Therefore, there were only a few New York firms capable of supplying fine, handmade jewelry in gold and platinum.

The purveyors of fine gemstones were the first to feel a need for such work again. While the cost of the metalwork was a fraction of the overall price of a jewel, a mounting in gold or platinum had, nevertheless, to be the best obtainable. Raymond C. Yard, Inc. and R. Esmerian Inc. were among the first jewelers to realize the potential, and they commissioned Carvin French to manufacture pieces for them.

The principals of Carvin French were not only master goldsmiths and platinum-smiths; they were also adept at enameling techniques, which were not well-known in America.

With his European background, Fulco di Verdura recognized the abilities of this workshop immediately. After his first meeting with André Chervin, Verdura went home and designed a series of new enamel jewels. The delicate, antique, painterly style that became associated with Verdura's work in the 1950s and early 1960s was, to a great extent, due to his collaboration with the master jewelers of Carvin French.

By the mid-1970s, Carvin French had stopped working in enamel, because it had become so popular that it was now mass-produced in the Orient. The firm had been investigating other materials since the late 1960s, trying to achieve highly colorful and unusual effects in jewelry, and it was concentrating heavily on lapidary work. Its workshop employed craftsmen capable of cutting and carving precious stones and semiprecious stones, which were produced for Donald Claflin and Angela Cummings of Tiffany & Co.

182. Two Jeweled Clocks
1986

Designed and manufactured by
Carvin French, Inc.
Lapis lazuli, rubies, rock crystal, topaz,
diamonds, enamel, and yellow gold

Changes in the Presentation of Women and Fashion

The early 1970s was another time of changing trends in American jewelry. As the decade opened, David Webb lamented, "The day of the million-dollar lady has passed—at least for the moment. Obvious jewels arouse resentment and inspire thieves. We are in a chaotic cycle and nondiamond jewelry seems casual and right."[1] Webb reacted to the times with a collection of rock-crystal jewelry set in gold and accented with small diamonds mounted in platinum.

By the middle of 1972, both Diana Vreeland and Nancy White, editors at *Vogue* and *Harper's Bazaar* respectively, had left their posts. James Brady was brought into *Harper's Bazaar* as publisher and editorial director; his first statement in 1971 sums up the new era, "And when we show fashion we will show it in more realistic settings, on real women. Ethereal studio settings and anonymous model girls leave me cold."[2] Gone was the photography shot in the far corners of the earth. Women were entering the business world.

The Italian jewelry firm Bulgari was on the verge of opening a branch in New York when one of its principals remarked on the change in American women and jewelry. "Women," said Gianni Bulgari, "are tired of curves. Even in stones they prefer rectangular-cut baguettes. . . . They no longer want something they put on or carry for great occasions, but jewelry they wear often with many things."[3]

Bulgari, New York

Bulgari opened their New York branch, Danaos Ltd., in the Pierre Hotel in 1971. Bulgari had been selling jewelry to Americans in Italy for the better part of the century (William Scheer, Inc. had been their agent in New York.) Notable Americans had been customers of the Roman establishment on Via Condotti as early as 1914, among them, the American "Copper King" William Boyd Thompson; the actor Gary Cooper, and the actress Kay Frances. At a time when leading American retail jewelers had passed out of family control and were accountable to a board of directors, Bulgari had the advantage of being steered by a family with a strong jewelry tradition going back to the nineteenth century. Bulgari also enjoyed a strong international following; so by the early 1970s, the firm was well aware of the changing market in America and of the desire for new jewelry.

Clockwise from top:

183. Pendant Necklace with Hinged Chain
1980s

Yellow sapphire, emerald, and yellow gold
Signed by Bulgari
Manufactured by Carvin French, Inc.

184. Brooches
1980s
Signed by Bulgari
Manufactured by Carvin French, Inc.
(top to bottom)

Fish with seaweed
Carved sapphire, rubies, and yellow gold

Flowers in a Pot
Hematite, rubies, yellow sapphire, diamonds, and yellow gold

Three Turtles
Blue and yellow carved sapphires, rubies, diamonds, emeralds, and yellow gold

185. Two Pairs of Earrings
1980s
Signed by Bulgari
Manufactured by Carvin French, Inc.
(top to bottom)

Emerald, yellow sapphire, cabochon rubies, hematite, diamonds, and yellow gold

Sapphires, rubies, hematite, and yellow gold

186. Miniature Lamp
(shown here illuminated)
1980s
(opposite)

Multicolored sapphire beads set with diamond pins, rubies, lapis lazuli, rock crystal, and yellow gold
Signed by Bulgari
Manufactured by Carvin French, Inc.

190

187. Necklace
1980s
(opposite)

Heart-shaped rubies, diamonds,
sapphire beads, and yellow gold
Signed by Bulgari
Manufactured by Carvin French, Inc.

188. Suite of Jewelry: Bracelet, Earrings, and Ring
1986

Canary and white diamonds, rubies,
emerald, and yellow gold
Signed by Bulgari
Manufactured by Carvin French, Inc.

189. Coin Necklaces on Link–chains
1980s
Signed by Bulgari
Manufactured by Carvin French, Inc.
(top to bottom)

Roman bronze coin depicting Emperor
Nerva (A.D. 96-98)
Rubies and yellow gold

Greek silver coin depicting Pagonia
Patras (111 B.C.)
Diamonds and yellow gold

American bronze coin depicting
George Washington (1795)
Diamonds, cabochon rubies, and
yellow gold

The Bulgari family spent their first few years in America testing the new market, observing the response of American women to their work, and listening to their clients' requests. Their American customers wanted jewels that were casual and wearable, yet sophisticated; something they would not have to change at various times of the day. This jewelry has since been called daytime-to-evening jewelry.

The Bulgari, New York style popularized yellow gold in a new way, reintroduced the rectangular baguette diamond (often custom-cut), and brought back the bezel-set cabochon, audaciously shown in profile. Bulgari, New York was also intrepid about putting antiquities in modern settings—antique coins and engraved gems, previously associated with ancient jewels and the archeological-revival jewels of the 1860s. Bulgari, New York presented these with solid gold chains. The result was clean, modern, polished—very romantic jewels that had an international appeal.

Donald Claflin at Bulgari, New York

Sensing that American women were bolder than their European counterparts, Bulgari, New York wanted to provide them with the look they desired. Great thought went into creating a concept for a jewel-around-the-clock. The firm soon realized that it would require a translator for its ideas, to give its jewels an American design touch. The artist-jeweler with this ability had his work in the Tiffany & Co. displays—the American jewelry designer Donald Claflin.

The arrival of Claflin at Bulgari, New York in 1976 set the scene for a revitalization of the jewelry field; Carvin French worked as Claflin's manufacturer. The association of Bulgari, New York, this designer, and Carvin French's workshop was one of the most felicitous in the recent history of jewelry.

The Bulgari, New York style took shape at a time when global fashion awareness was beginning to peak. The response to the new jewelry was universally positive in the fashion centers of the world. The presence of Bulgari, New York jewels in New York, Palm Beach, Paris, Gstaad, St. Tropez, etc. was soon pervasive and gave the family the recognition previously accorded only to courturiers of the stature of Christian Dior. The byproduct of the enormous success of this house was a renewal of interest in America in all precious jewelry.

Afterword

190. Necklace
1984

Engraved emerald, heart-shaped
multicolored sapphires, diamonds,
pearl drop, platinum, and yellow gold
Manufactured by Carvin French, Inc.
for R. Esmerian, Inc.

Americans have been consistently buying jewelry since the nineteenth century, and their desire for the finest gems and jewelry available has kept the gem-trading centers focused on New York. The depletion of the ancient sources of rare precious gemstones or interruptions in mining have made the collections already amassed in America very significant and desirable.

The American jewelry industry has benefited, in each successive era since the Civil War, by the immigration of groups of skilled foreign craftsmen, merchants, and gifted designers. America's cities have been host to Europeans wishing to profit from the wealth of American connoisseurs.

The eagerness of Americans to own beautiful jewelry of high intrinsic value is an internationally established fact. Their corresponding delight in wearing fashionable up-to-date pieces has proved a challenge to retailing jewelers and jewelry designers alike and has prompted technical innovations in the jeweler's workshop with far-reaching consequences. Moreover, the mobility of America's democratic society has kept precious jewelry from remaining in the hands of a select few, and these changes in ownership have generated stylistic renewals.

The demand for precious jewelry continues in the United States to this day. The requirements for achieving success as a jeweler have proved to be an ability to obtain precious materials, an accompanying awareness of trends in international markets, an understanding of technical applications and the ability to direct them, as well as great imagination and courage in running a business.

Clockwise from top:

191. Earrings
1982

Cabochon emerald, diamonds, yellow
gold, and platinum
Manufactured by Carvin French, Inc.
for R. Esmerian, Inc.

192. Pendant Earrings
1984

Emerald drops, diamonds, cabochon
rubies, and yellow gold
Manufactured by Carvin French, Inc.
for R. Esmerian, Inc.

193. Brooch
1981

Ruby, sapphire, emerald, canary and
white diamonds, and yellow gold
Manufactured by Carvin French, Inc.
for R. Esmerian, Inc.

194. Necklace
1983

Cabochon emerald, diamonds, and
platinum
Manufactured by Carvin French, Inc.
for R. Esmerian, Inc.

195. Fox Necklace
1985

Pearls, ruby and ruby beads,
diamonds, and platinum
Pearls and ruby beads woven by
Hilda Janssens of R. Esmerian, Inc.

196. Emerald Elephant Necklace
1984

Cabochon rubies and ruby beads,
diamonds and diamond beads,
carved emerald, pearls, yellow gold,
and platinum
Pearls and ruby beads woven by
Hilda Janssens of R. Esmerian, Inc.
Manufactured by Carvin French, Inc.
for R. Esmerian, Inc.

197. Necklace

1977

(opposite)

Oval-cut sapphires and sapphire
beads, diamonds, and platinum
Manufactured by Albert J. Pujol, Inc.
for R. Esmerian, Inc.

Albert J. Pujol, Inc. (formerly Vors &
Pujol, Inc.) was formed by members of
the Cartier workshop in 1967 and
moved out of the Cartier building to
18 West Fifty-sixth Street in 1982.

198. Necklace

1984

Emerald drops, canary and white
diamonds, yellow gold, and platinum
Manufactured by Carvin French, Inc.
for R. Esmerian, Inc.

Notes

Introduction

1. *The Jewelers' Circular and Horological Review* (New York, October, 1879): 165.
2. *Ibid.*

Chapter One

1. *The Jewelers' Circular and Horological Review* (New York, August 22, 1917): 83.
2. *Jewelers' Circular* (May, 1890): 74.
3. *Jewelers' Circular* (October 25, 1899): 9.
4. Walton S. Webb, ed., *Webb's Historical, Industrial and Biographical Florida*, New York: W.S. Webb & Co., 1885, p. 148.
5. *Jewelers' Circular* (December 13, 1899): 1.

Chapter Two

1. *The New York Daily Tribune*, October 5, 1861.
2. *The Jewelers' Circular and Horological Review* (New York, February, 1894): 19.
3. *Ibid.*
4. Samuel Eliot Morison, Henry Steele Commager, William E. Leuchtenburg, *A Concise History of the American Republic*, New York: Oxford University Press, 1977, p. 285.

Chapter Three

1. *The Jewelers' Circular and Horological Review* (New York, February, 1894): 19.
2. *Jewelers' Circular* (September, 1878): xviii, xix.
3. *Ibid.*
4. *Ibid.*
5. Carlo M. Cipolla, *The Technology of Man*, New York: Holt, Rhinehardt & Winston, 1980, pp. 199–200.
6. *Jewelers' Circular* (February, 1879): 6.
7. *Jewelers' Circular* (December, 1887): 393.
8. *Jewelers' Circular* (November 22, 1899): 50.

9. *Jewelers' Circular* (April, 1889): 29.
10. *Ibid.*
11. *Ibid.*, p. 30.
12. *Ibid.*, p. 29–30.
13. *Jewelers' Circular* (January 19, 1927): 47.
14. *Ibid.*
15. *Jewelers' Circular* (October 11, 1893): 21.
16. *Ibid.*
17. H. Clifford Smith, *Jewellery*, New York: Putnam's, 1908, pp. 338–40.

Chapter Four

1. Robert Koch, *Louis C. Tiffany: Rebel in Glass*, New York: Crown Publishers, 1966, p. 65.
2. *The Jewelers' Circular and Horological Review* (New York, August 15, 1901): 1.
3. Cecil Beaton, *The Glass of Fashion*, New York: Doubleday & Co., 1954, p. 141.
4. *Ibid.*
5. *Ibid.*
6. *Jewelers' Circular* (October 16, 1907): 57.
7. *Jewelers' Circular* (November 20, 1907): 73.
8. *Jewelers' Circular* (August 4, 1915): 68.
9. *Jewelers' Circular* (July 19, 1916): 50.
10. *Jewelers' Circular* (August 16, 1916): 59.

Chapter Five

1. *The Jewelers' Circular and Horological Review* (New York, April 24, 1912): 85.
2. *Jewelers' Circular* (November 23, 1918): 51.

Chapter Six

1. *The Metropolitan Museum of Art Bulletin* (New York, March, 1920): 51.
2. *The Jewelers' Circular and Horological Review* (New York, February 6, 1907): 125.

3. Jessica Daves, *Ready-Made Miracle*, New York: Putnam's, 1967, p. 51.
4. Arthur J. Pulos, *American Design Ethic: A History of Industrial Design*, Cambridge, Mass.: MIT Press, 1986, p. 304.
5. *Report of Commission to International Exposition of Modern Decorative and Industrial Art in Paris, 1925*, Washington, D.C.: U.S. Department of Commerce, 1925, p. 62.
6. *Ibid.*
7. *New York American*, Sunday, March 22, 1925.
8. *Vogue* (New York, July 15, 1917): 85.
9. *Atlanta Journal*, May 11, 1923.

Chapter Seven

1. *Vogue* (New York, March 15, 1935): 73.
2. *The Jewelers' Circular and Horological Review*, (New York, March, 1934): 42, 45, 126.
3. Personal communication: Louis Tamis.
4. *Harper's Bazaar* (New York, February, 1934): 37.
5. *Ibid.*
6. *Town and Country* (New York, November, 1937): 67f.
7. *Harper's Bazaar* (New York, May, 1936): 106.

Chapter Eight

1. *Vogue* (New York, December 15, 1942): 46f.
2. *Ibid.*

Chapter Nine

1. Personal communication: Maurice Galle.
2. *Vogue* (New York, April 15, 1910): 16.

Chapter Ten

1. *The Jewelers' Circular and Horological Review* (New York, January, 1937): 53, 55.
2. Personal communication: Julius Cohen.

Chapter Twelve

1. Personal communication: Stanley Silberstein.
2. *Vogue* (New York, March 15, 1964): 125.
3. *Ibid.*
4. *Vogue* (New York, June, 1964): 112.

Chapter Thirteen

1. *Stockton, California Record*, June 9, 1970.
2. *Harper's Bazaar* (New York, November, 1971): 81.
3. *New York Post*, September 1, 1970, p. 7.

Glossary

Acid Etching The production of a design through the use of acid, a caustic chemical that attacks the surface of metal.

Bangle Bracelet A rigid bracelet that can be slipped on the arm, or hinged, or clasped.

Baroque Pearl A freshwater or oceanic pearl that is irregularly shaped.

Bezel Setting A type of setting composed of a band of metal that encircles a gem and holds it in place.

Blister Pearl A nacreous excrescence on the inside of a mollusk shell.

Box Pin A brooch of some depth, frequently designed to hold a lock of hair and a miniature.

Bric-a-brac An eclectic collection of fashionable, decorative objects for the house.

Cabochon A rounded, unfaceted stone with a polished surface.

Carat Gold Gold with measured increments of copper, silver, and other alloying metals.

Casting The processes of making molds and utilizing them to shape metal.

Chasing The shaping, decorating, or finishing of a metal surface using hammer and tools on the front of the piece.

Cleaving A process for splitting diamonds into two or more parts that are subsequently recut and polished to make the finished gems.

Clip Brooch A brooch that can be fastened by a variety of devices that grip, clasp, or hook.

Cold Chiseling The process of decorating unheated metal using a hammer and tools with cutting edges.

Conch Pearl A nacreless, pink-orange concretion formed by the conch.

Demantoid Garnet A garnet of an extraordinary green color that was mined in the Ural Mountains of Russia in the late nineteenth century.

Enamel Powdered glass colored by metallic oxides and fused to metal.

Engine-turned A technique of decorating metal with a lathe.

Fancy-cut Gem Cuts that produce shapes other than round.

Flexible Box Bracelet A multiple-unit bracelet with hinges, capable of bending.

French-cut Gem A square cut that originated in France.

Guilloche Enamel Transparent enamel applied to metal that has been ornamented with a machine-generated pattern of multiple lines.

Handy Pin A small brooch, decorative and utilitarian, used to hold scarves, lace, bonnet ribbons, or shawls in place.

Hard Solder A solder containing copper; requires high heat to melt.

Hardstone Inlay Semiprecious stones in a mosaic pattern.

Investment The refractory material used to make a mold.

Invisible Setting A gem setting with no metal visible.

Jobbing Houses Establishments made up of individuals who do work by the piece, act as middlemen, and do business within the wholesale trade.

Kimberlite Pipe A columnlike mass of igneous rock that contains diamonds; located in Kimberley, South Africa.

Kunzite A pink variety of spodumene named for George Frederick Kunz.

Line Bracelet A thin bracelet which, when not in use, lies flat.

Link-chain A succession of multiple rings forming a chain.

Lost-wax Casting Casting utilizing a wax model, which melts when heat is applied, and is replaced by the molten metal during casting.

Mouth Blowpipe A tubular device into which one blows for the purpose of directing and increasing heat from a stationery flame.

Novelty A small decorative or utilitarian object, distinguished by its new and unique design.

Oriental Pearl A natural marine pearl.

Oxidation The effect of oxygen on metal: discoloration.

Oxy-gas Blowpipe A late nineteenth-century term used to describe a torch deriving its flame from a mixture of oxygen and fuel gas in a fixed proportion.

Painted Enamel Finely ground enamel painted over a previously enameled surface and fused into place.

Paste A crystal glass with a high lead content, used in the manufacture of imitation gems.

Patination A coloration caused by the action of chemicals on the surface of metal.

Pictorial Bracelet A wide bracelet with abstract and representational designs.

Pinchbeck A zinc-copper alloy used in the manufacture of imitation gold jewelry.

Plique-à-jour Enamel Transparent enamel in a pierced metal framework; has the appearance of stained glass.

Precious Topaz The name for true topaz.

Repoussé Work The process of shaping metal using hammer and tools on the reverse side of the piece.

Silverware A term applied to all objects made in silver with the exception of jewelry.

Slave Bracelet A link-chain bracelet derived from Egyptian prototypes.

Spodumene A type of gem; a lithium aluminum silicate that occurs in prismatic crystals, often of great size.

Star Sapphire A sapphire which, when cut as a cabochon, displays a star.

Turbo Shell A marine snail, having a turban-shaped shell with a pearly lining.

Vanity Case A portable, decorated case for cosmetics.

Vinaigrette A small, decorated bottle for holding an aromatic preparation: scent or smelling salts.

General Bibliography

The following periodicals have been perused from their first dates of publication: *The Jewelers' Circular and Horological Review; The National Jeweler;* New York; *Vogue;* New York; *Harper's Bazaar;* New York; *Town and Country,* New York.

We found *The Jewelers' Circular and Horological Review* to be the best available source about the pioneers in American jewelry, the formation of their companies, and the development of technology in this field. The *National Jeweler* was invaluable for its coverage of the Depression years through World War II. The fashion magazines were informative on styles and attitudes.

For the general historical framework, we have drawn on Morison, Commager, and Leuchtenburg's text, *A Concise History of the American Republic. Only Yesterday and Since Yesterday* has provided invaluable insight into the 1920s and 1930s.

C.H. Carpenter's two books, *Gorham Silver* and *Tiffany Silver,* were sound historical guides to these great American firms. *The Tiffany Touch* was a well researched text and also helpful. *Selling Quality Jewels Since 1800: A History of Shreve, Crump & Low Co.* gave a coherent history of that Boston firm and its founding families.

By necessity we have read widely; below we list those texts which provided accurate information pertinent to the analysis and writing of our history.

Allen, Fredrich Lewis. *Only Yesterday and Since Yesterday.* New York: Bonanza, 1986.

Beaton, Cecil. *The Glass of Fashion.* New York: Doubleday, 1954.

Bovin, Murray. *Centrifugal or Lost Wax Jewelry Casting.* Forest Hills, N.Y.: Bovin Publishing, 1977.

Carpenter, Jr., Charles H. *Gorham Silver, 1831-1981.* New York: Dodd, Mead & Co., 1982.

——— and Carpenter, Mary Grace. *Tiffany Silver.* New York: Dodd, Mead & Co., 1978.

Chase, Edna Woolman and Chase, Ilka. *Always in Vogue.* New York: Doubleday, 1954.

Cipolla, Carlo M. and Birdsall, Derek. *The Technology of Man.* New York: Holt Rinehart & Winston, 1980.

Daves, Jessica. *Ready-Made Miracle.* New York: Putnam's Sons, New York, 1967.

Davison, Lonnelle. "Platinum in the World's Work." In: *National Geographic Society Magazine* (September, 1937): 345-66.

"E. Colonna." Essay by Martin Eidelberg. Dayton: The Dayton Art Institute. (October 29, 1983–January 2, 1984).

Gaal, Robert. *Diamond Dictionary.* Santa Monica, Ca.: Gemological Institute of America, 1977.

Hoke, C.M. *Testing Precious Metals.* New York: Jewelers' Technical Advice Company, 1946.

Hurlbut, Jr., Cornelius and Switzer, George S. *Gemology.* New York: John Wiley & Sons, 1979.

Ingram, J. S. *The Centennial Exposition.* Philadelphia: Hubbard Bros., 1876.

Krashes, Laurence S. *Harry Winston: The Ultimate Jeweler.* New York and Santa Monica, Ca.: Harry Winston, Inc. and the Gemological Institute of America. 1984.

Koch, Robert. *Louis C. Tiffany: Rebel in Glass.* New York: Crown, 1966.

Legrand, Jacques. *Diamonds: Myth, Magic, and Reality.* New York: Crown, 1980.

L'Exposition des Arts Décoratifs 1925. Paris, 1926.

Mcdonald, Donald. *A History of Platinum.* London: Johnson Matthey & Co. Ltd., 1960.

Marcus, Stanley. *Minding the Store: A Memoir.* Boston: Little, Brown, 1974.

Morison, Samuel Eliot; Commager, Henry Steele; and Leuchtenburg, William E. *A Concise History of the American Republic.* New York: Oxford University Press, 1977.

Nadelhoffer, Hans. *Cartier: Jewelers Extraordinary.* New York: Harry N. Abrams, 1984.

Pulos, Arthur J. *American Design Ethic: A History of Industrial Design.* Cambridge, Mass.: MIT Press, 1986.

Purtell, Joseph. *The Tiffany Touch.* New York: Random House, 1971.

Ringsrud, Ron. "The Coscuez Mine: A Major Source of Colombian Emeralds." In: *Gems and Gemology* (Summer, 1986): 67-79.

Report of Commission to International Exposition of Modern Decorative and Industrial Art in Paris, 1925. Washington, D.C.: Department of Commerce, 1925.

Selling Quality Jewels Since 1800: A History of Shreve, Crump & Low Co. Boston, 1974.

Selwyn, Arnold. *The Retail Jeweller's Handbook.* London: Heywood & Co. Ltd., 1948.

Smith, Cyril Stanley. *A Search for Structure.* Cambridge, Mass.: MIT Press, 1981.

Untracht, Oppi. *Jewelry Concepts and Technology.* New York: Doubleday, 1982.

Vreeland, Diana. *D.V.* New York: Vintage Books, 1984.

Webster, Robert. *Gems: Their Sources, Descriptions, and Identification.* London: Butterworths, 1962.

Index